WRITTEN IN EXILE:
THE POETRY OF LIU TSUNG-YUAN

Also by Red Pine/Bill Porter

Travel Writings (as Bill Porter)

Road to Heaven: Encounters with Chinese Hermits
The Silk Road: Taking the Bus to Pakistan
South of the Clouds: Travels in Southwest China
Yellow River Odyssey
Zen Baggage: A Pilgrimage to China

Chinese Poetry

Cathay Revisited
The Collected Songs of Cold Mountain
Guide to Capturing a Plum Blossom by Sung Po-jen
In Such Hard Times: The Poetry of Wei Ying-wu
The Mountain Poems of Stonehouse

Chinese Poetry Anthologies

*The Clouds Should Know Me by Now: Buddhist
Poet Monks of China* (with Michael O'Connor)
*Poems of the Masters: China's Classic Anthology
of T'ang and Sung Dynasty Verse*

Buddhist, Zen, and Taoist Texts

A Day in the Life: The Empty Bowl and Diamond Sutras
The Diamond Sutra: The Perfection of Wisdom
The Heart Sutra: The Womb of Buddhas
The Lankavatara Sutra: Translation and Commentary
*Lao-tzu's Taoteching: With Selected Commentaries
from the Past 2,000 Years*
The Platform Sutra: The Zen Teaching of Hui-neng
P'u Ming's Oxherding Pictures and Verses
Stonehouse's Poems for Zen Monks
Trusting the Mind: Zen Epigrams
The Zen Teaching of Bodhidharma
*The Zen Works of Stonehouse: Poems and Talks
of a Fourteenth-Century Chinese Hermit*

柳宗元

Written in Exile:
The Poetry of
Liu Tsung-yuan

TRANSLATED BY RED PINE

COPPER CANYON PRESS
PORT TOWNSEND, WASHINGTON

Cover art: Photograph by Bill Porter

Copper Canyon Press is in residence at Fort Worden State Park
in Port Townsend, Washington, under the auspices of Centrum.
Centrum is a gathering place for artists and creative thinkers
from around the world, students of all ages and backgrounds,
and audiences seeking extraordinary cultural enrichment.

LIBRARY OF CONGRESS CATALOGING-IN-PUBLICATION DATA
Names: Liu, Zongyuan, 773–819, author. | Red Pine, 1943– translator.
Title: Written in exile : the poetry of Liu Tsung-Yuan / Red Pine
  [translator].
Description: Port Townsend, Washington : Copper Canyon Press, [2019]
Identifiers: LCCN 2019013658 | ISBN 9781556595622 (paperback : alk. paper)
Subjects: LCSH: Liu, Zongyuan, 773-819—Translations into English. | Chinese
  poetry—221 B.C.-960 A.D. —Translations into English.
Classification: LCC PL2673 .A2 2019 | DDC 741.5/973—dc23
LC record available at https://lccn.loc.gov/2019013658

9 8 7 6 5 4 3 2 FIRST PRINTING

COPPER CANYON PRESS
Post Office Box 271
Port Townsend, Washington 98368
www.coppercanyonpress.org

For Li Xin and Yin Yun

Contents

ILLUSTRATIONS

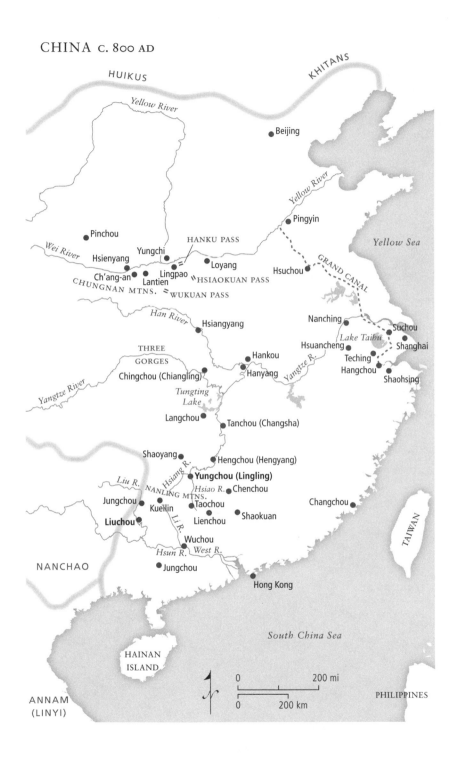

CHINA c. 800 AD

HUIKUS

KHITANS

Yellow River

Beijing

Yellow River

Pingyin

Yellow Sea

Pinchou

Wei River

HANKU PASS

Hsienyang   Yungchi

Ch'ang-an   Lingpao   Loyang   Hsuchou

Lantien

CHUNGNAN MTNS.   HSIAOKUAN PASS

WUKUAN PASS

GRAND CANAL

Han River   Hsiangyang

Nanching

Hsuancheng   Lake Taihu   Suchou

THREE

GORGES

Chingchou (Chiangling)

Hankou

Hanyang   Yangtze R.

Teching   Shanghai

Hangchou

Shaohsing

Yangtze River

Tungting

Lake

Langchou   Tanchou (Changsha)

Shaoyang

Hengchou (Hengyang)

Liu R.   NANLING MTNS.   Yungchou (Lingling)

Hsiao R. Chenchou

Jungchou   Kueilin   Taochou

Li R.

Liuchou   Lienchou   Shaokuan

Changchou

TAIWAN

Wuchou

Hsun R.   West R.

NANCHAO   Jungchou

Hong Kong

South China Sea

HAINAN

ISLAND

N

0   200 mi

ANNAM

(LINYI)

0   200 km

PHILIPPINES

PREFACE

I'M SURPRISED TO BE WRITING THIS. Two years ago, I pretty much decided to stop writing books, thinking it was time to do something else, like nothing. But two years before that, while I was pouring whiskey on the graves of Chinese poets and writing *Finding Them Gone*, I discovered Liu Tsung-yuan 柳宗元 (*Pinyin:* Liu Zongyuan). I had never read much of his poetry. Other than the handful of verses included in different translations of *Three Hundred Poems of the T'ang* 唐詩三百首, there wasn't much in English. And I didn't come across any more than that in Chinese. He was better known for his prose. I only included him in my travel itinerary after reading online accounts by his descendants searching for his grave. I love looking for things and thought wandering across the countryside south of Sian 西安 would at least make an interesting excursion. And so I started reading his poems. It didn't take long before I felt somewhat abashed that I had overlooked him. But I wasn't alone. Ever since the Chinese started ranking their literary giants, they have ranked Liu Tsung-yuan as one of the two greatest prose writers of the T'ang, the other being his friend and colleague, Han Yu 韓愈. One reason his poetry wasn't given equal billing was that there is so little of it. The standard edition of his complete works includes only 146 *shih*-style 詩 poems, a drop in the bucket for most major T'ang poets. Li Pai 李白 and Tu Fu 杜甫 each left over a thousand, and Pai Chu-yi 白居易 over three thousand. Overshadowed by the attention given to his prose, Liu's poetry was simply overlooked. At least it was until the Sung-dynasty poet Su Tung-p'o 蘇東坡 discovered it.

If anyone is responsible for putting Liu's poetry on an equal footing with his prose, it was Su, who wrote that the T'ang poets he would rank after Li Pai and Tu Fu would be Wei Ying-wu 韋應物 and Liu Tsung-yuan, which would make Liu one of the four greatest poets of the T'ang, in addition to being one of its two greatest writers of prose. Having previously translated Wei Ying-wu's poems, I shouldn't have been surprised to find myself agreeing with Su. Once I finished *Finding Them Gone*, I began messing around with Liu's poems—and I never intended to do more than mess. It didn't take long before I realized I couldn't stop. Here it is two years later, and this is what I've got to show for it, instead of all those do-nothing days I had planned—and to which I hope I can now return.

In addition to being captivated by Liu's poetry, I was impressed by the man and by how he came to write what he did. His work is unique in that he wrote nearly everything that has survived while he was living in exile in the far south of China. He spent the last fifteen years of his life a thousand miles from home and died when he was only forty-seven. It wasn't prison, but it wasn't home, and so he wrote. And anyone who has read what he wrote is glad he did.

For those hoping to serve as officials in ancient China, writing was a job requirement. The civil service exam demanded a high level of ability in both prose and poetry—prose for reports, memorials, inscriptions, and letters; poetry for meeting or saying goodbye, for offering congratulations or commiseration, for banquets, or for sitting alone in the moonlight, but whatever the occasion, for expressing what was in one's heart. Still, whether they were writing poetry or prose, educated Chinese such as Liu didn't think of themselves as essayists or poets. They were officials first and foremost. And while Liu lived and worked in the capital, he wrote like an official, about government policies and events involving the administration. And he was very good at this. People sought him out— even the emperor. But I wasn't interested in reading the memorials on policy he wrote for presentation at court or the inscriptions he wrote for special occasions or the letters about recent goings-on. It was the poetry that drew me in. The poetry was personal. It made me want to know more about the man who wrote it. Now that I'm done, I think people who read the translations in this book will also want to know more about the person who wrote the poems, and this is what I've learned.

In 773, the same year Charlemagne was laying siege to towns in northern Italy, and the Indian zero was being introduced to the mathematicians of the newly built city of Baghdad, Liu Tsung-yuan was born in the Chinese city of Ch'ang-an 長安. One more mouth to feed among the city's two million others. Two decades earlier, the An Lu-shan Rebellion 安史之亂 (755–763) had destroyed much of the city. It had recovered, but the central government had survived only by relying on foreign mercenaries and on regional military forces headed by men who paid lip service but not necessarily tax revenues to Ch'ang-an. Had it not been for the government's control of the salt trade, which accounted for half its revenue, it would not have lasted another decade, much less 250 more years. But at least things in the capital were more or less back to normal. And at least Liu was born into a good family. His mother was a Lu 盧. The Lus of Fanyang 范陽 (just south of Beijing) were one of the five great families of the T'ang and had supplied the court with a number of chief ministers during the dynasty's early years. They also produced the dynasty's greatest Zen master, Hui-neng 惠能 (638–713), whose father was a Lu, albeit a banished one.

Liu Tsung-yuan's father also came from an important family. His branch of the Liu clan traced its ancestry back fifteen hundred years and thirty-nine generations to a man named Chan Huo 展獲 (720–621 BC). Chang spent his days sitting under a willow in the Yellow River town of Pingyin 平陰 dispensing advice, not far from where Confucius 孔子 would later do the same. People started calling him Liu-hsia-hui 柳下惠, the Wise Man under the Willow, and the name stuck. Eventually one branch of his descendants moved west from the Yellow River floodplain to where the river came down from Inner Mongolia and turned east just past the town of Yungchi 永濟. The place they chose was Pupan 蒲坂, where the Su River 涑水 joined the Yellow. Two thousand years earlier, this was also the location chosen by Emperor Shun 舜帝 for his capital. It was a strategic place, being one of only five fords on the Yellow. The move by the Liu clan was apparently prompted by the shift in the center of power at the end of the Chou dynasty 周代 from Loyang 洛陽 to Hsien-yang 咸陽, where the Ch'in dynasty 秦代 established its capital in 221 BC. It was only a three-day ride west from Pupan to Hsienyang, on the north shore of the Wei River 渭河, and later on to Ch'ang-an on its south shore. In the centuries that followed, no dynasty went by without at least a few Lius serving in the higher echelons of court bureaucracy. During the long reign of the T'ang-dynasty emperor Kao-tsung 高宗 (r. 649–683), twenty-two members of the Liu family served in the Department of State Affairs 尚書省, which was where business at court got done.

The senior member of the family at that time was Liu Shih 柳奭 (d. 659), whose niece was Empress Wang 王皇后, which should have been a good thing. And it was, until Kao-tsung became enamored of a woman named Wu Chao 武曌. Wu Chao had been a concubine of Kao-tsung's father, Tai-tsung 代宗 (r. 626–649). When an emperor died, the normal procedure was for his concubines to become nuns and to move into the western part of the palace, effectively putting them out of the reach of palace affairs. If Wu Chao became a nun, she didn't stay a nun. Three years after Tai-tsung died, she bore Kao-tsung a son. She then murdered her own daughter—fathered by Tai-tsung—and blamed it on the empress. Kao-tsung believed her and demoted Empress Wang. He then elevated his father's former concubine to become his new empress, Empress Wu. Empress Wang's principal supporter had been her uncle, Liu Shih, who had served as one of the chief ministers at court for years. When Empress Wang fell, so did Liu. He was demoted and then banished and finally murdered on his way back to the capital to be tried for his "crimes."

That marked the end of high times at court for the Lius. They continued to serve, but not at the upper level. Liu Tsung-yuan's great-grandfather Liu Tsung-yu 柳從裕 never served higher than city magistrate, neither did his grandfather Liu Ch'a-kung 柳察躬. Liu's father, Liu Chen 柳鎮 (739–793), did a bit better, perhaps because he married a Lu. Shortly after his marriage, he too became a magistrate. In his case, the city of which he was put in charge was Ch'ang-an itself. Things were looking up for the Lius. And things looked positively rosy in 773 after Liu Chen's wife gave birth to a son. She had already given birth to two daughters, but a family's prestige and wealth came through its sons. Both parents were thirty-four at the time, and this was their last child. They called the boy Tsung-yuan. This was the name by which he was known to his family and friends. The formal name he acquired when he turned twenty and by which he was referred to by the public was Tzu-hou 子厚. He was also sometimes called Ho-tung 河東, after the location of his ancestral home: east of where the Yellow River comes down from North China.

At the time of his birth, Liu's parents were living in the capital's Chin-jen ward 親仁里, which bordered the southwest corner of the city's East Market. The market was huge, a kilometer on a side. It was where the upper class shopped and lived. Hence, it was a good place to grow up— not that such things would have mattered to a child. But this changed in 777. Liu's grandfather, Liu Ch'a-kung, died in Suchou 蘇州, just west of the mudflats that would later become Shanghai 上海. It was a long way away, but the Lius were devoted followers of Confucian traditions, one of which required a three-year period of mourning for the death of a parent. Being the eldest of five sons, Liu's father quit his post and traveled to Suchou to take care of funeral arrangements. After the funeral, instead of returning to Ch'ang-an, Liu Chen decided to spend the mourning period in Suchou. It turned out Liu Ch'a-kung was a local hero. Before he retired and moved to Suchou, his last post was as magistrate of nearby Teching 德清. The people of Teching were so grateful, they built a shrine in his honor, and he became their city god. The people of Teching still carry his statue through the streets every year to honor his memory.

Meanwhile, back in the capital, with her husband in mourning and not receiving a salary, Liu's mother no longer had sufficient means to support herself and her children and moved to the countryside west of the capital to some farmland the Lu family owned on the Feng River 灃河. This was where Liu Tsung-yuan grew up and the place he later recalled in his poems when he thought of home. He was going on five, and it was also time for him to begin his education, at least the rudimentary phase. Since there wasn't enough money for a tutor, his mother became his teacher. During their move she had neglected to bring any books with her, so she had to rely on her memory. But she was an educated woman, and what she remembered were the "Odes" in the *Shih-ching* 詩經, or Book of Poetry. And so Liu Tsung-yuan's education began with poetry—poetry and messing around in the garden.

When, in 780, Liu Chen completed the three-year period of mourning, instead of returning to Ch'ang-an he asked to be appointed magistrate of Hsuancheng 宣城, south of Nanching 南京. It wasn't any closer to the capital, but Liu Chen had lived in Hsuancheng as a teenager when he and his mother hid out there during the An Lu-shan Rebellion. Something about their time together drew him back. And at least the appointment included a salary that allowed him to provide his wife and children with the means to move back into the city. Liu Tsung-yuan was nearly eight, and his regular studies finally began, again under his mother's guidance, but now with the help of a library of three thousand volumes his grandfather had left behind in the care of his other sons. Liu began to read the classics, be they Confucian, Taoist, or Buddhist, and by all accounts he was a precocious student.

The young Liu's studies, however, were interrupted three years later. In the fall of 783, troops brought from western China to restore order in other parts of the country mutinied. They took over the capital, and the emperor and his court had to flee. Earlier that year, Liu's father's three-year appointment in Hsuancheng ended, and he was appointed magistrate of Lingpao 靈寶, just across the Yellow River, more or less, from the Liu ancestral home near Yungchi. During the mutiny, Liu's mother sent her son to join his father, while she stayed in the capital with her two daughters.

Once the insurrection was put down in the summer of 784, the court returned, and Liu's father was rewarded for his service, and his loyalty. He was appointed administrative assistant to the military training commissioner for a vast region that included the areas south of the middle reaches of the Yangtze 長江. This time he took his son with him. Liu Chen's job required him to visit all the major cities in the region, and he began with Hankou 漢口, where the Han River 漢江 joins the Yangtze. From there he proceeded south up the Hsiang River 湘江 to Changsha 長沙. While he was there, he arranged for his son, who was now twelve, to be betrothed to a daughter of the Yang 楊 family, a family that had already supplied a wife to Tu Fu and that would later supply one to Pai Chu-yi. During these peripatetic years, Liu Tsung-yuan attended local Confucian academies whenever possible, but he and his father never spent more than a year in any one place, and he often studied with tutors or on his own, under, of course, his father's guidance.

Finally, in 788, when Liu was almost sixteen, his father was recalled to Ch'ang-an and rewarded for his service with the prestigious post of assistant censor in the Censorate 御史臺. Liu Tsung-yuan, meanwhile, began preparing for the exams he hoped would open the door to his own career as an official. As in his previous assignments, Liu's father displayed an unwavering sense of justice. His first year at his new post, he was given charge of retrying a case and was instrumental in having the previous verdict overturned. The chief minister Tou Shen 竇參 was furious, as he had been responsible for applying the pressure that had resulted in the original verdict. For his temerity, Liu Chen was banished to the Yangtze Gorges and remained there for three years until Tou Shen himself was banished. Upon Liu Chen's return in 792, he was rewarded for his refusal to bow to pressure and was appointed attendant censor in the Censorate, one notch higher than his previous post as assistant censor.

During his father's absence, Liu dutifully took the imperial exams every year. But as the son of a man banished by someone as powerful as

Tou Shen, it was hopeless. It was not until Tou Shen himself was banished that Liu Tsung-yuan passed, with honors. It was the second month of 793, and he was twenty-one years old.

With his son's future looking bright and his own as well, Liu Chen decided it was time to conclude his son's marriage to the daughter of the Yang clan to whom his son was betrothed nine years earlier. Unfortunately, Liu's father died in the fifth month of that year—he was only fifty-four, and the marriage had to be postponed.

Although the customary three-year period of mourning prevented the young Liu from accepting an appointment in the government, it didn't mean he had to stay home. He joined his father's brother in the border post of Pinchou 邠州, 100 kilometers northwest of the capital. His uncle was serving there as administrative assistant to the military commissioner. During his years studying for the exams, Liu had formed relationships with a number of officials in the capital, and it hadn't taken long for them to notice his literary skills. Even though Liu was "in mourning" and living in a military encampment in a border region, they began asking him to write compositions, including drafts of memorials they hoped to present at court. Liu was thus able to put his sabbatical to good use, which laid the groundwork for his future rapid rise through the ranks.

When the mourning period ended in 796, Liu returned to Ch'ang-an and consummated his marriage to his betrothed. He was twenty-four, and she was twenty. On his return, he also received an appointment as an assistant in the palace library. It wasn't much of a post, but it provided an income and allowed Liu to prepare for another exam, a special one held later that year for recruiting especially talented men. Liu failed, but when the exam was held again two years later, he passed. He finally received his first real appointment. He became a proofreader in the Academy of Scholarly Worthies 集賢殿書院, which was responsible for compiling works for the palace library. It marked not only the beginning of Liu's career as an official, but also the beginning of his literary career. His talents had already been noticed while he was a student and later while he was in mourning. He now became a sought-after writer of compositions of all kinds.

Liu was not only gaining a reputation as a writer, his reasoning abilities caught the notice of a group of reform-minded officials headed by Wang Shu-wen 王叔文 (753–806), who was chief adviser to the crown prince, Li Sung 李誦. It was also around this time that Liu and his mother moved into his grandfather's former residence in the Shanho ward 善和里 (the name was changed to the Hsinglu ward 興祿里 in the T'ang, but Liu always refers to it by the old Sui-dynasty name). It was directly opposite the main gate of the Forbidden City and couldn't have been a more prestigious address. But whatever joy Liu experienced in life was invariably soon balanced with sorrow. The first year at his new post, his wife had a miscarriage, and the following year she died giving birth to a stillborn infant. We don't know much about Liu's relationships with other women, but two years later, in 801, he fathered a daughter with an unknown woman. Perhaps she was a singsong girl Liu met at one of the parties the literati were always attending. He called his daughter Ho-niang 和娘, Happy Girl, and she lived with him the rest of her all-too-brief life.

Liu's three-year appointment to the Academy ended the same year his daughter was born. It would have been normal for him to be sent out to the provinces then as a magistrate—to round out his experience with a local assignment. But Wang Shu-wen and the crown prince wanted to keep Liu close by—Liu later described his role in this group as its "secretary." Wang arranged for Liu to be appointed commandant in charge of military affairs in the nearby town of Lantien 藍田. It was only 60 kilometers southeast of the capital, but Liu didn't have to go even that far. It wasn't a real appointment. The metropolitan governor at the time was Wei Hsia-ch'ing 韋夏卿. Wei's authority encompassed the entire Ch'ang-an area, including Lantien, and he arranged for Liu to work in his office as a secretary so that he could continue taking part in meetings with Li Sung and Wang Shu-wen and drafting memorials for the crown prince to submit to the emperor.

Two years later, in the tenth month of 803, Liu's Lantien appointment ended and he was "recalled" to the capital. This time he was appointed investigating censor in the Censorate. It was a major step up the bureaucratic ladder. He was joined there by Han Yu, the other great prose writer of the T'ang, and Liu Yu-hsi 劉禹錫, who would also become a major poet, as well as Liu's literary executor. Liu Tsung-yuan wasn't quite thirty, but already he was conferring regularly with the group of advisers gathered around the crown prince and was making friends throughout the court.

A year later, in the winter of 804, Li Sung suffered a stroke that left him partially paralyzed and unable to speak. It changed the nature of the group's meetings, but its members continued to draft proposals for the crown prince to give to his father, Emperor Te-tsung 德宗 (r. 780–805). Two months later, in the first month of 805, Te-tsung died, and Li Sung, despite his partial paralysis, ascended the throne as Emperor Shun-tsung 順宗. Wang Shu-wen moved quickly and had the members of their group appointed to senior positions. Liu Tsung-yuan became a vice director of the Ministry of Rites, and his friend Liu Yu-hsi a vice director of the Department of State Affairs. These were heady titles but really beside the point. As they began implementing the policies they had discussed over the previous five years with the crown prince, their influence stretched into all areas of the court.

At heart, these policies were meant to curtail—if not end—a wide variety of forms of corruption and usurpation of privilege. They were chiefly aimed at limiting the power of the regional governors and the palace eunuchs and strengthening the power of the central government. Among other things, they included dismissing and charging corrupt officials, reforming the tax code, ending collusion between local officials and state monopolies, and getting rid of "palace shopping," whereby eunuchs or their henchmen entered shops and took whatever they wanted.

The entrenched officials at court and the more powerful eunuchs naturally opposed these policies aimed squarely at them. They conspired with other officials, who were now being left out of the decision-making process, to bring all this to an end. Things happened fast. In the fifth month of 805, less than four months after becoming emperor, Shun-tsung was forced to make his eldest son, Li Ch'un 李純, crown prince. Then in the eighth month, he was forced to abdicate, while his son became Emperor Hsien-tsung 憲宗 (r. 806–820). In addition to putting an end to the reforms, Hsien-tsung banished all those who took part, which, of course, included Liu. Wang Shu-wen had already left Ch'ang-an in the sixth month when his mother became ill. Shortly after he arrived at the family home in far off Shaohsing 紹興, she died, and he began the three-year period of mourning. A few months later, at the beginning of the following year, he was given permission to commit suicide.

Meanwhile, in the ninth month of 805, the eight men who formed the core of the reform movement were exiled, among them Liu Tsung-yuan and Liu Yu-hsi. All eight were appointed magistrates of posts in

South China. Liu's post was in Shaochou 邵州 (modern Shaoyang 邵陽) in Hunan province, and he left a week later with his sixty-seven-year-old mother, his four-year-old daughter, a nurse, two cousins, and his friend and fellow reformer Liu Yu-hsi. Because Liu Tsung-yuan's mother was ill, they decided against the shorter, more difficult route through the Chungnan Mountains 終南山 via the Wukuan Pass 武關. Instead, they traveled east through the Hanku Pass 函谷關 and then took the easier Hsiaokuan Pass 崤關 south. From there, the route took them overland, across the Yangtze, then across Tungting Lake 洞庭湖. While on their way, they learned that the emperor had decided he had been too lenient. Their assignments were changed. Liu Yu-hsi's new post was actually an improvement. It was changed from far-off Lienchou 連州 to Langchou 郎州, just west of Tungting Lake. Liu Tsung-yuan, however, was ordered 100 kilometers farther south to Yungchou 永州. But the emperor's point wasn't the location, it was the job. They were all demoted to the mere functionary post of assistant magistrate. They would have nothing to do, which was excruciating punishment for men whose lives had been concerned with reforming the government.

After the Liu entourage crossed Tungting Lake, they continued up the Hsiang River and stopped in Tanchou 潭州 (Changsha) to visit Liu Tsung-yuan's father-in-law, Yang P'ing 楊凭. Yang was serving not only as town magistrate but also as governor of the entire West Chiangnan Circuit 西江南道, which included Yungchou, Langchou, Chenchou 郴州, Taochou 道州, and half a dozen other outposts. Liu Yu-hsi then headed west to his post in Langchou, and Liu Tsung-yuan continued south to Yungchou, another 250 kilometers upstream to where the Hsiang was joined by the Hsiao River 瀟河.

The prefecture toward which Liu and his family were traveling included 25,000 square kilometers of forests and farmland and a tax-paying population of 150,000. It had been brought into the Chinese orbit centuries earlier, and its population consisted mostly of Han Chinese. But it also included a mixture of Chuang 壮, Miao 苗, Yao 瑤, and Tung 侗—ethnic groups that had previously occupied the river valleys but had been forced into the hills by migrations of Han Chinese. Finally, in the last month of the year, eighty days after leaving Ch'ang-an, Liu reached the Hsiao River town of Yungchou. His post not only didn't include any responsibilities or authority, it didn't include a place to live. Fortunately for Liu, this wasn't a problem. His mother was a devout Buddhist, and he himself had long been interested in the Dharma. The abbot of Lunghsing Temple 龍興寺 welcomed them. Liu's two cousins later found lodging across the river, but for Liu the monastery became his home for the next five years.

Less than a month later, at the beginning of 806, the emperor announced a new reign period and a general amnesty, which extended to all exiles except the Eight Assistant Magistrates 八司馬, as they were called. It didn't take long for Liu to realize he was going to be in Yungchou for a while, and the wind that once filled his sails died. For the first time he experienced depression. As spring gave way to summer, his mother's illness worsened, and she died. Liu arranged for her body to be sent back and buried in the family graveyard south of Ch'ang-an on the Chifeng Plateau 棲鳳原. Now it was just himself, his daughter, and a nursemaid.

There was a bright side, though, to being an assistant magistrate. It was a forced vacation, and Liu began to take advantage of it. He spent his time hiking through the countryside, drinking with like-minded individuals, and writing whatever came to mind. Inspiring him were friends who joined him there, as well as his two cousins. Liu Tsung-chih 柳宗直 was his cousin on his father's side and became the brother he never had. Tsung-chih had also passed the imperial exam but decided he would rather accompany his cousin than wait for the unlikely prospect of an appointment. Lu Tsun 盧遵 was his cousin on his mother's side and was a constant companion, not only in Yungchou but also at Liu's next place of exile. Other friends included Wu Wu-ling 吳武陵, who passed the imperial exam in 807 but was banished to Yungchou the following year, and Yuan K'e-chi 元克己, who was another regular at evening get-togethers and on excursions. Also, Liu's maternal uncle, Ts'ui Min 崔敏, arrived and served as magistrate of Yungchou from 808 until 810. Considering the circumstances, Liu couldn't have been better off. The group that gathered around him became so famous, it was talked about in the capital, and would-be officials came from far afield to study with him. Liu was just as famous for his calligraphy as he was for what he wrote.

Most periods of exile in China ended after two years or at the most five. When the five-year mark went by with no reprieve, Liu concluded he was never going back. Some days he identified with Ch'u Yuan 屈原 (340–278 BC), the exiled poet whose laments he knew by heart and to which he responded with his own sense of unjust banishment. Other days he identified with T'ao Yuan-ming 陶淵明 (365–427), the poet who retired from government service early enough to enjoy life as a farmer, and Liu began to plant things.

Once the five-year mark passed, Liu decided to move out of the monastery and to build a hut across the river. He didn't exactly take up farming, but he did lead the life of a retired gentleman. Once again, just as he was getting settled, sorrow visited. His daughter, Happy Girl, succumbed to illness. Before she died, she asked her father if she could become a nun. She was only ten, but Liu arranged for her to be ordained, and she took the name Ch'u-hsin 初心, Beginner's Mind. Another reason Liu might have moved out of the monastery was that he had formed a relationship with a local peasant woman. She became his de facto wife and gave birth to another daughter a year after Beginner's Mind died.

The place Liu chose for his new home was on a tributary of the Hsiao. It was called the Janhsi River 冉溪, but Liu soon changed the name. He reasoned that he was living in Yungchou because he was so stupid, that it was his stupidity that had led him to oppose the eunuchs and other entrenched officials at court. He renamed the stream the Yuhsi 愚溪, or Stupid River, and he lived what had to be the happiest years of his life on or near its banks. The site of his initial residence has since become a shrine, but this wasn't the only place he lived. At some point Liu built a second, larger residence near the mouth of Stupid River on land now occupied by the town's Number-Seven High School. Being right next to the ferry made it easier for his friends to visit and for him to visit them. Also, it was a relatively flat piece of land and provided more room for planting things. Liu planted hundreds of trees while he was in Yungchou, especially orange trees.

Although Liu lived the life of a retired gentleman, he was not the sort of person who slept late or went to bed early. He explored every nook and cranny in the area, and he received constant requests to compose inscriptions and drafts of memorials others hoped to submit at court. While he was in Yungchou, he maintained correspondence with hundreds of people. Liu still hoped to serve in some capacity, and he wrote countless appeals to others hoping they might help put an end to the disregard, if not enmity, the holders of power felt toward him.

Finally, in the first month of 815, Liu was recalled, along with Liu Yu-hsi and three other members of the original eight—two of whom had died, and one of whom had simply retired. Liu hurried back to Ch'ang-an and arrived less than six weeks later in the third week of the second month. He arrived full of hope. But the hope didn't last long. The long shadow that had scuttled the careers of other members of the Liu family was still at work. Their return had been orchestrated by Wei Kuan-chih 韋貫之, one of the court's two chancellors. But the court's other chancellor was Wu Yuan-heng 武元衡, a great-grandson of the Liu-family nemesis, Empress Wu. Wu Yuan-heng bore the group of reformers a grudge, as they had rebuffed his attempts to join them. He should have been happy he didn't! But when the chancellor heard someone recite "The Peach Blossoms of Hsuantu Temple" 玄都觀桃花 (see poem 114 in *Poems of the Masters*), which Liu Yu-hsi wrote shortly after his return, about visiting a Taoist temple and seeing all the peach trees planted since he was exiled, Wu (and others) interpreted the poem as critical of the government. Three weeks after they returned, the five surviving assistant magistrates were exiled again. This time they were elevated to posts as magistrates, but their new posts were even farther from the capital than before. In Liu's case, his new assignment was to Liuchou 柳州, just north of Vietnam.

In the middle of the third month, Liu and his friend Liu Yu-hsi left Ch'ang-an once more. Six weeks later, they said goodbye halfway up the Hsiang in the town of Hengyang 衡陽. Liu Yu-hsi continued overland across the Nanling Mountains 南嶺山 to his new post in Kuangtung province, and Liu Tsung-yuan continued up the Hsiang, then through the Lingchu Canal 靈渠 to the Kuei River 桂江 (aka Li River 漓江) and down the Kuei to the Hsun 潯江, and finally up the Hsun and Liuchiang 柳江 Rivers to Liuchou. He arrived at the end of the sixth month, more than three months after setting out.

If Yungchou was a provincial backwater, Liuchou was barely a town. The prefecture, not the town but the prefecture, had a population of 7,000 compared to Yungchou's 150,000. And those who spoke Chinese were few and far between. Life was very different. Child slavery was common, and during his tenure Liu personally redeemed over a thousand children who had been sold to pay off debts. He continued to write, producing some of his best work. But he finally had responsibilities, and he devoted himself to carrying them out. In this, he had the support of P'ei Hsing-li 裴行立, magistrate of Kueichou 桂州 and governor of the region that included Liuchou.

Liu made a deep impression on the people of Liuchou, just as his grandfather had on the townspeople of Teching. Unfortunately, Liu's health was failing. He was suffering from beriberi and constipation, and he contracted cholera. He struggled on for four years. Finally, in the eleventh month of 819, he was recalled once more. But the reprieve came too late. Before he could pack, he died. He was forty-seven. Knowing he didn't have long to live, he wrote to his friend Liu Yu-hsi, asking him to serve as his literary executor. It was Liu Yu-hsi who, in 822, put together the first collection of Liu Tsung-yuan's surviving works. Governor P'ei took care of the funeral arrangements, and Liu's cousin Lu Tsun accompanied the body back to the family cemetery, where it was buried alongside that of Liu's mother on the Chifeng Plateau south of the capital. Liu's epitaph was written by his friend and colleague, Han Yu. It appears in this book after the poems. Lu Tsun also took care of Liu's son, born shortly after Liu Tsung-yuan arrived in Liuchou, and a second son born shortly after he died. One of the sons—no one knows which—eventually passed the imperial exam and became an official, but nothing more is known about him.

Also in 822, three years after Liu died, the townspeople of Liuchou constructed a memorial grave and a shrine to honor his memory. The shrine and grave are still there, along with descendants of Liu's ubiquitous orange trees and the pond he was fond of visiting when the heat became unbearable. Although Liu didn't become a city god like his grandfather, he did become the city's hero and its face to the outside world. Most people assume the town was named for him.

That pretty much sums up what I've learned about Liu Tsung-yuan's life. In the notes that I've appended to his poems, I'll be repeating most of it, as I've always been of the opinion that without understanding the background of a poem it's impossible for a translator to do it justice, and why shouldn't the reader share in this knowledge?

In trying to describe Liu's poems, I defer once again to Su Tung-p'o. Su wrote, "Of those poets whose work looks lifeless but is full of vitality, whose appearance is plain but whose essence is beautiful, that would be T'ao Yuan-ming and Liu Tsung-yuan" 其外枯而中膏，似澹而實美，淵明子厚，之流也. It was a beauty in no small part born of his circumstances. At the age of thirty-two Liu was banished. He had time on his hands. What he wrote in Ch'ang-an was bureaucratic in nature. What he wrote in Yungchou and Liuchou was about life, albeit life in exile. During the fifteen years he spent a thousand miles from home, he produced some of China's greatest literature. His essays became the model later writers sought to emulate, and the ideas he expressed became a staple of thinkers, regardless of their points of view. He wrote in every genre, and with equal skill. He was as well known for his prefaces and inscriptions as he was for his allegories and fables or his memorials and letters. He even invented a new genre, the travel journal, with which I particularly identify, having honed such literary skills as I possess by doing two-minute pieces of fluff for an English-language radio station in Hong Kong about my own journeys in the Middle Kingdom. Had I read his work earlier, I might have cut down on the fluff. Also, Liu didn't restrict himself to the standard Confucian view of things. He was equally at home with Taoist and Buddhist ways of looking at the world. And he wrote more or less as he might have talked, free and easy, but always in a style that elevated his work above his contemporaries'.

It's hard to know how writers come to write the way they do. Liu's mother, no doubt, played an important role, as his father was absent from the time he was four until he turned eleven. But his father played an equally important, if different, role, as Liu accompanied him between the ages of eleven and sixteen on his missions south of the Yangtze. During this time, the young Liu studied with tutors and attended local academies, but he was often left to his own devices, and he was free to choose his own literary models. Instead of the convoluted, ornate style that had become popular with officials over the previous 1,000 years, Liu looked to writers who weren't simply stylists but also had something to say. He modeled himself and his writing on the works of Mencius 孟子, Chuang-tzu 莊子, and Ssu-ma Ch'ien 司馬遷 and the historical commentaries of the *Tsochuan* 左傳. Critics later labeled what he developed as the ancient, or *ku-wen* 古文, style and contrasted it with the *p'ien-wen* 駢文, or parallel, style that had dominated literary genres from 200 BC until the T'ang. Liu cast aside the formal elements that often overshadowed a work's content in favor of communicating ideas and feelings directly; he also had fun with the language in which he did so. I can only hope my translations give some sense of the ease with which he wrote.

In the pages that follow, I've included 140 of the 146 regular *shih*-style poems Liu left behind. I've omitted six that have a combined length of over 500 lines and would have required a small book of notes as well as more enthusiasm than I was likely to muster. I haven't bothered with Liu's ten *fu*-style 賦 prose poems or his nine *sao*-style 騷 laments, as they were written in a manner that the rest of his literary output argues against: dense as mud and weighed down by endless historical references. I've also ordered the poems in a chronological sequence, as near as can be ascertained or guessed at. Naturally there are differences of opinion about the dates of certain poems, but such differences are almost always limited to one or two years. I've also interspersed the poems with twenty of the prose pieces Liu wrote about his places of exile along with a few of his more popular allegories and fables and one letter. I've numbered these with uppercase roman numerals.

The texts I've used for the poems and the prose and have reproduced in this book are those in the four-volume Collected works of Liu Tsung-yuan 柳宗元集 published by the China Publishing Company in 1979 as part of its Chinese Ancient Literature Text Collection 中國古典文學基本叢書. Where I've chosen variants of any significance, I've indicated that in my notes. Also, at the end of each note, I've indicated in parentheses the page number where readers can find the original text in the above edition.

Lastly, in preparing this book, I've had the good fortune to visit the places where Liu wrote these poems and prose pieces and to spend time with local scholars who have devoted themselves to his work. I am indebted to them for much of the information in this book. I'm not a scholar, and they saved me from having to become one. For readers interested in learning more, at the back of this book I've listed some of these scholars' works along with the few English-language sources available. My thanks, too, to my traveling companions, Yin Yun 殷雲 and Li Xin 李昕, who helped arrange my visits to Liu's places of exile and who joined me on my excursions. After coming up empty searching for Liu's grave south of Sian, I never would have guessed I would find him still alive.

Red Pine
Summer 2018
Port Townsend

Written in Exile:
The Poetry of Liu Tsung-yuan

1. ON SEEING THE PAINTING *FESTIVE CLOUDS* AT THE EXAMINATION 省試觀慶雲圖詩

Before colors were added shapes were drawn
through diaphanous clouds the capital appeared
celestial blessings bestowed from on high
assembled officials offering felicitations
on his robe a dragon embraced the sun
untouched by the royal censer's smoke
His Eminence surveyed the horizon
his gaze extended into space
while his radiance shone forth from the scroll
the splendors of the auspicious scene were unrolled
a lasting example of Emperor Yao's virtue
instead of riverine art a celebration

設色初成象，卿雲示國都。九天開秘祉，百辟贊嘉謨。
抱日依龍袞，非煙近御爐。高標連汗漫，向望接虛無。
裂素榮光發，舒華瑞色敷。恆將配堯德，垂慶代河圖。

....

NOTE: Written in Ch'ang-an in 790. This is Liu's earliest extant poem. He was only eighteen, but it already shows his admiration for the ways of China's early sage kings—an admiration that endured throughout his career as an offical and his subsequent exiles. The painting of the imperial court he describes was used as the subject of the civil service exam that year. The emperor was considered the Son of Heaven, and the image of a dragon playing with the sun was a common motif on royal robes. Among the sage rulers the Chinese revered were Emperor Yao 堯 (ca. 2350 BC) and Fu Hsi 伏羲 (ca. 2850 BC). Fu Hsi was once given by the Dragon King of the Yellow River a set of diagrams on the basis of which he composed the trigrams that made up the earliest version of the *Book of Changes* 易經. As a result of the enmity borne Liu's father by the prime minister, Tou Shen, Liu failed the examination the previous year, and he failed this year too, and the next year, and the next. Finally, on his fifth attempt, when the prime minister himself was exiled, he passed in 793 at the age of twenty-one. His friend Liu Yu-hsi also passed that year. (1261)

2. The Turtle Shell Game 龜背戲

The game first appeared in Ch'ang-an in the palace
the sound soon filled the homes of nobles
gold coins falling on jade plates
turtle shells polished like an autumn sky
sacred symbols marking the eight directions
up and down and six different ways
someone spins a magical device
stars fly and clouds break apart
then come together again
who can tell what exists and what doesn't
suddenly things scatter and disappear
then in a flash it's all like before
everything of course rises and falls
but a single move here decides victory or defeat
old-style chess is no longer in vogue
whims of the past are disdained by the times
if more than luck lights its occult lines
may it grant my lord a thousand years
but serving as an altarpiece isn't for me
the idle rich indulge in all sorts of things

長安新技出宮掖，喧喧初徧王侯宅。玉盤滴瀝黃金淺，皎如文龜麗秋天。
八方定位開神卦，六甲離離齊上下。投變轉動玄機卑，星流霞破相參差。
四分五裂勢未已，出無入有誰能知。乍驚散漫無處所，須臾羅列已如故。
徒言萬事有盈虛，終朝一擲知勝負。修門象棋不復貴，魏宮粧奩世所棄。
豈如瑞質耀奇文，願持千歲壽吾君。廟堂巾笥非余慕，錢刀兒女徒紛紛。

....

NOTE: Written in Ch'ang-an shortly before 800 while Liu was still in his
twenties. Serving at court, Liu came into contact with the goings-on among
the excessively rich and idle. Here he describes a new board game that had
become fashionable. Judging from the description, the lines on the turtle
shell formed the "board," and elements of chance were involved but also auto-
matic writing, as in the modern Ouija board. It was about this time that such

writing first appeared among Taoists. In his self-titled book (17.11), the Taoist sage Chuang-tzu turns down an offer to be a minister at court and compares such an opportunity to the choice given a turtle of having its shell used in the ceremonies of the king or of continuing to wag its tail in the mud. The turtle, of course, was known for its long life. (1248)

I. THE JUNK BUG 蝜蝂傳

Junk bugs are insects that like to carry things. Whenever they encounter something, they grab it, then lift it with their heads onto their backs. No matter how heavy or troublesome it might be, they don't quit. Because their backs are rough, whatever they pile on top doesn't fall off. When they finally collapse and can't get up, if someone takes pity on them and removes their burden, as soon as they can move, they pick it up again and continue on as before. They're also fond of climbing heights and do so with all their might until they fall to their deaths.

Likewise, there are people today so greedy they don't let anything of value escape without adding it to their possessions. They don't consider how burdensome it might be, only that they might fail to acquire it. But the moment they're careless and trip, they suffer the misfortune of dismissal or banishment. And yet, as long as they can get back up, they continue on unrepentant. Every day they wonder how to improve their position or how to increase their salary, and their greed grows to the point where they approach ruin. Even if they should consider how those who came before them have perished, they don't stop. Although they appear great, and we call them "men," they possess the intelligence of insects. This is truly sad.

蝜蝂者，善負小蟲也。行遇物，輒持取，卬其首負之。背愈重，雖困劇不止也。其背甚澀，物積固不散。卒躓仆不能起，人或憐之，為去其負，苟能行，又持取如故。又好上高，極其力不已，至墜地死。

今世之嗜取者，遇貨不避，以厚其室。不知為己累也，唯恐其不積。及其怠而躓也，黜棄之，遷徙之，亦以病矣。苟能起，又不艾。日思高其位，大其祿，而貪取滋甚，以近於危墜。觀前之死亡，不知戒。雖其形魁然大者，其名人也，而智則小蟲也。亦足哀夫。

....

NOTE: Although this reflects Liu's impression of people he met in Ch'ang-an, this was most likely written while he was himself banished and living in Yungchou. This insect is usually identified as the larval stage of the green lacewing, or ant lion, which piles the bodies of ants it has killed on its back for camouflage. Liu has broadened its habits a bit here to serve the purposes of allegory. (483)

3. Wei Tao-an 韋道安

Tao-an was a Confucian scholar
equally skilled with a bow or sword
traveling through the Taihang Mountains at twenty
one evening he heard someone cry
spurring his horse to investigate
he found an old man in a disheveled state
"I was a county official," he said
"but I was demoted and returning to Ch'ang-an
when suddenly bandits attacked me
they didn't leave me a thing
I don't mind losing my possessions
they took my daughters too
before I knew it they were gone
who knows if my girls are dead or alive
I may as well end this life
how can I face another day"

道安本儒士，頗擅弓劍名。二十遊太行，暮聞號哭聲
疾驅前致問，有叟垂華纓。言我故刺史，失職還西京。
偶為群盜得，毫縷無餘贏。貨財足非恡，二女皆娉婷。
蒼黃見驅逐，誰識死與生。便當此殞命，休復事晨征。

Tao-an's sense of injustice was roused
his eyes narrowed and his body tensed
he grabbed his bow and asked where they went
in a matter of minutes he was over the ridge
he saw the bandits beside a stream
they were arguing among themselves
with a single arrow he killed the leader
the others yelled out in fright
he told them to tie up each other
then to put the rope in his hands
the two girls had given up hope
they were expecting a gruesome end

they cowered and wouldn't come closer
he told them to follow him back to their father
then slinging the stolen goods over his shoulder
he hurried back to where he set out

一聞激高義，眥裂肝膽橫。掛弓問所往，趫捷超崢嶸。
見盜寒澗陰，羅列方忿爭。一矢斃酋帥，餘黨號且驚。
麾令遞束縛，縲索相拄撐。彼姝久褫魄，刃下俟誅刑。
卻立不親授，論以從父行。捃收自擔肩，轉道趨前程。

he made a fire that night with his flint
the forest was bright as day
the old man and his daughters embraced
their tears mixed with their blood
the father bowed and offered his goods
he told the girls to call Tao-an "husband"
Tao-an straightened his robe and left
justice is precious and profit a trifle
the ancients disparaged rewards such as marriage
families shouldn't form due to arms
he left to practice the scholarly arts
for ten years he was thus engaged
until Prefect Chang of Hsuchou
came waving his banner at the palace gate
devotion to a cause was Tao-an's goal
he left Ch'ang-an and rode forth

夜發敲石火，山林如晝明。父子更抱持，涕血紛交零。
頓首願歸貨，納女稱舅甥。道安奮衣去，義重利固輕。
師婚古所病，合姓非用兵。竭來事儒術，十載所能逞。
慷慨張徐州，朱邸揚前旌。投軀獲所願，前馬出王城。

he distinguished himself at his post
but autumn winds rose on the Huai
his lord suddenly died
and those he commanded rebelled
defying the emperor's mandate

they filled the land with sounds of war
their excesses couldn't be contained
their defiance couldn't be restrained
lifting his head Tao-an drew his sword
those who love justice don't think of themselves
not that martyrs are oblivious of death
they die to remain loyal and true
while others die fighting for power
or spend their lives chasing glory
my song isn't meant to mourn a man's death
but to mourn the ways of this world

轅門立奇士，淮水秋風生。君侯既即世，麾下相敬傾。
立孤抗王命，鐘鼓四野鳴。橫潰非所壅，逆節非所嬰。
舉頭自引刃，顧義誰顧形。烈士不忘死，所死在忠貞。
咄嗟徇權子，翕習猶趨榮。我歌非悼死，所悼時世情。

....

NOTE: Written in Ch'ang-an in the summer of 800, when Liu was serving as proofreader in the Academy of Scholarly Worthies. There was an insurrection that year in the Huai River region. When Chang Chien-feng 張建封, the magistrate of Hsuchou 徐州, died, the rebels made Chang's son the new magistrate and refused to accept the court's orders to put down their weapons. Chang had visited Ch'ang-an in 797 looking for talented men to assist him, and Wei Tao-an took up his banner. Unwilling to accept the flaunting of imperial authority, Wei committed suicide in protest. The loss of imperial control over the appointment of regional governors and their successors also meant loss of revenue for the court and was the single most serious problem facing the T'ang government during Liu's lifetime. In the case of Hsuchou, it meant loss of control over the transshipment of grain coming from the Yangtze via the Grand Canal. Liu wrote a prose piece to accompany this poem, but it has since been lost. (1206)

4. At Chief Minister Hun's Residence on Hearing a Song Resembling "White Linen" 渾鴻臚宅聞歌效白紵

A breathtaking beauty parts kingfisher curtains
in the light of a fall moon a dragon blade is unsheathed
crimson lips whisper without making a sound
gold pipes and jade chimes echo from the palace
inciting the sky to lower the autumn heat
turning the sun to crystal in a world without bounds
and these goblets of wine, again, why are we drinking

翠帷雙卷出傾城，龍劍破匣霜月明。朱脣掩抑悄無聲，金簧玉磬宮中生。
下沉秋火激太清，天高地迴凝日晶。羽觴蕩漾何事傾。

....

NOTE: This fancy poem depicts the highlights of an evening at the minister's residence and was written in Ch'ang-an sometime before Liu's exile in the ninth month of 805. Hun Chien 渾鍼 was the minister in charge of vassal state ceremonials. An odd number of lines was unusual in Chinese poetry, but Liu is emulating the seven-line song "White Linen" in which the rhyme is carried by the second, fourth, sixth, and seventh lines. The second line here refers to a sword dance, and the pipes in the fourth line were made of metal and consisted of half a dozen or more vertical tubes. Clearly, by the time he was thirty, Liu's skill as a poet transcended the versification common among court officials. Unfortunately, we have only these four examples of his early work. (1250)

5. ODE FOR A CAGED EAGLE 籠鷹詞

In whistling wind and pelting sleet
an eagle takes off in morning light
flying through clouds cutting through rainbows
it dives like lightning into the hills
slicing through thickets of thorns with its wings
it grabs a rabbit then flies into the sky
other birds scatter from its bloody talons
settling on a perch it surveys its realm
the hot winds of summer suddenly arise
it loses its feathers and goes into hiding
harassed by vermin lurking in the grass
frightened and distressed unable to sleep
all it can think of is the return of cool air
escaping its restraints and soaring into the clouds

凄風淅瀝飛嚴霜，蒼鷹上擊翻曙光。雲披霧裂虹蜺斷，霹靂挈電捎平岡。
砉然勁翮剪荊棘，下攫孤兔騰蒼茫。爪毛吻血百鳥逝，獨立四顧時激昂。
炎風溽暑忽然至，羽翼脫落自摧藏。草中狸鼠足為患，一夕十顧驚且傷。
但願清商復為假，拔去萬累雲間翔。

....

NOTE: Written in Yungchou, most likely in the twelfth month of 805 shortly
after Liu arrived at his place of exile. We have no poems about his departure
from Ch'ang-an or his journey. He was either too depressed or too preoc-
cupied with taking care of his mother. She was ill and died the following
summer. Although Liu was not imprisoned, his exile came with restrictions
on his movements. It was a new experience, and the eagle's confinement
reminded him of his own predicament. The eagle in this case is one that has
been raised from a chick and trained to hunt. Such birds are kept in a pen
during the summer molting period while their flight feathers are growing
out again. (1246)

6. ODE FOR A ONE-FOOTED CROW 跂烏詞

Dawn lights the walls and all the crows fly
cawing and fighting over the sunniest branches
preening their feathers they seem happy
why are you alone glum today
did your love of heights lead you too near the sun
did the three-footed one hurt you out of spite
or were you hungry and cawing at the roadside
when someone decided to try a new kind of meat
my puny-winged one-footed friend in the bushes
grabbing low branches pulling yourself up with your beak
looking down in the mud for ants and crickets
and up at roof beams to guard against swallows
your wings might be as sharp as knives
but unable to jump you can't fly high
No Toes and Crippled Legs weren't affected
try to fly low and you'll avoid further harm

城上日出群烏飛，鴉鴉爭赴朝陽枝。刷毛伸翼和且樂，爾獨落魄今何為。
無乃慕高近白日，三足妬爾令爾疾。無乃飢啼走路旁，貪鮮攫肉人所傷。
翹肖獨足下叢薄，口銜低枝始能躍。還顧泥塗備螻蟻，仰看棟梁防燕雀。
左右六翮利如刀，踽身失勢不得高。支離無趾猶自免，努力低飛逃後患。

....

NOTE: Written in Yungchou most likely at the end of 805, shortly after Liu
arrived. Cutting off the feet was a common punishment for criminals in
ancient China. Although exile was hardly the same, Liu identifies with the
one-footed crow. According to an ancient myth, a three-footed crow lives on
the sun—crows being especially fond of shiny things. In this case, the shiny
thing is the emperor, and the light is his grace, over which the black-robed offi-
cials fight every morning at court. In the penultimate line, Liu mentions two
disabled men who appear in *Chuangtzu* (5.3 & 5.5) as examples of those who
suffered a physical deformity yet were able to rise above it due to their unim-
paired moral qualities. Chuang-tzu's text also includes numerous examples
of survival, if not longevity, that resulted from keeping a low profile. (1244)

II. THE BEAR 羆說

Deer are afraid of wildcats, wildcats are afraid of tigers, and tigers are afraid of bears. Covered with long shaggy hair and able to stand upright, bears possess exceptional strength and are capable of killing people. In the south of Ch'u there once was a hunter who could make all kinds of animal calls with his flute. One day he took his bow and arrows and his firepot into the mountains, and he made a call to attract deer. He waited, and when a deer appeared, he started a fire, then he shot the deer. But when a wildcat heard the deer call, it came too. The hunter was terrified and pretended to be a tiger to frighten it. But when the wildcat ran off, a tiger appeared. The man was even more terrified and pretended to be a bear. The tiger disappeared. But a bear heard the call and came looking for a mate. When it saw the man, it grabbed him and tore him apart and ate him. It turns out that those who rely on external aids instead of developing what they have within themselves invariably end up as bear food.

鹿畏貙，貙畏虎，虎畏熊。熊之狀，被髮人立，絕有力甚害人焉。楚之南有獵者，能吹竹為百獸之音。嘗云持弓矢罌火而即之山，為鹿鳴以感其類。伺其至，發火而射之。貙聞其鹿也，貙而之。其人恐，因爲虎而駭之。貙走而虎至，愈恐，則又為熊，亦亡去。熊聞而求其類，至則人，捽搏挽裂而食之。今夫不善內而恃外者，未有不為熊之食也。

....

NOTE: The ancient kingdom of Ch'u 楚 included the region to which Liu was exiled. The firepot referred to here was an oil lamp and was used to start fires to drive animals toward hunters. (467)

7. THE FIRST PLUM FLOWERS 早梅

Plum flowers appear first on the taller trees
shining in the distance against the blue southern sky
the North Wind diffuses their scent at night
heavy frost at dawn adds to their white
I wish I could send them a thousand miles
but with so many mountains and rivers in between
these wintertime blossoms would surely fade
how could they console a distant friend

早梅發高樹，迴映楚天碧。朔吹飄夜香，繁霜滋曉白。
欲為萬里贈，杳杳山水隔。寒英坐銷落，何用慰遠客。

....

NOTE: Written in Yungchou in the first month of 806. The last four lines
reprise a poem by Lu K'ai 陸凱 (198–269): "Meeting a courier I broke off a
branch / I'm sending it to a friend on the northern border / finding nothing
else south of the Yangtze / this branch of spring will have to do." 折花逢驛
使，寄與隴頭人。江南無所有，聊贈一枝春. Liu was an incurable realist, not a
romantic. (1233)

8. Thinking of My Old Garden in Spring 春懷故園

The sound of bureau birds is late
it's time for spring farmwork in Ch'u
I keep thinking of the water in my old pond
waiting for someone to irrigate the garden

九扈鳴已晚，楚鄉農事春。悠悠故池水，空待灌園人。

....

NOTE: Written in Yungchou at the beginning of 806. Newly arrived at his place of exile, Liu still expects to return to Ch'ang-an and thinks back to where he grew up as a boy southwest of the capital along the Feng River. Originally the term "bureau birds" referred to an ancient division of government into nine bureaus, each named for a different bird and in charge of overseeing a different aspect of the agricultural calendar. Here, in the domain of the ancient state of Ch'u, the local bureaucrats are sleeping late. Living in exile and serving as a deputy magistrate with no responsibilities or authority, Liu not only can't assist the farmers in Yungchou, his talents are ignored by those empowered to do so. (1264)

9. Meeting a Farmer at the Start of Spring 首春逢耕者

Spring arrives early in southern Ch'u
things start to grow while it's cold
the power of the earth is loose in the land
hibernating creatures are stirring
there's no color yet in the countryside
but farmers are already plowing
I can hear birds singing in the orchards
I can see springs flowing in the marshes
farming of course is honest work
but an exile is cut off from normal life
my old pond I imagine is overgrown
the family farm all thorns and vines
I would be a hermit but I'm not free
nothing I try succeeds
I related all this to a farmer
explaining my situation in detail
he kept rubbing the handle of his plow
and turning to look at the looming clouds

南楚春候早，餘寒已滋榮。土膏釋原野，百蟄競所營。
綴景未及郊，積人先耦耕。園林幽鳥囀，渚澤新泉清。
農事誠素務，羈囚阻平生。故池想蕪沒，遺畝當榛荆。
慕隱既有繫，圖功遂無成。聊從田父言，款曲陳此情。
眷然撫耒耜，迴首煙雲橫。

....

Note: Written in Yungchou in the spring of 806. Yungchou was located in the southernmost part of the ancient state of Ch'u, whose territory included the north and south sides of the middle reaches of the Yangtze. The home Liu refers to was not where he lived just outside the palace in Ch'ang-an but the place that belonged to his mother's family. It was a few kilometers southwest of the city between the Feng River and the Shaoling Plateau 少陵 and was where he spent his childhood. After his death, Liu's body was taken back to the capital and was buried on the plateau not far from where the poets Tu Mu 杜牧 and Wei Ying-wu 韋應物 were buried. This begins like a T'ao Yuan-ming poem, but it doesn't end that way. Instead of expressing a desire to join the farmer, Liu remains a banished official wishing he could return to court. (1212)

10. Reading Zen Texts in the Morning at Transcendent Master Temple
晨詣超師院讀禪經

Gargling with well water makes my teeth chatter
after purifying myself I brush off my clothes
I happened to pick up a palm-leaf text
leaving the east wing I kept reading
"There's nothing to find in the wellspring of truth"
"What the world follows are the footprints of falsehood"
I wish I could fathom those ancient words
will I ever be done perfecting my nature
the monastery courtyard is quiet
it's all green moss and bamboo
sunny days the fog and dew linger
the pine trees look just washed
the peace I feel is hard to describe
I'm happy just being awake

汲井漱寒齒，清心拂塵服。閒持貝葉書，步出東齋讀。
真源了無取，妄跡世所逐。遺言冀可冥，繕性何由熟。
道人庭宇靜，苔色連深竹。日出霧露餘，青松如膏沐。
澹然離言說，悟悅心自足。

....

NOTE: Written in Yungchou in the summer of 806, when Liu would have been new to a monastic environment. Such was the insignificance of Liu's post, it didn't include government lodging, but Buddhist temples often provided rooms for visiting officials. Lunghsing Temple was a five-minute walk east of the Hsiao River and just below the west-facing slope of Chienchiuling 千秋嶺, which formed the southeast border of the city. The temple's grounds are now home to the city's tax bureau and a primary school. Liu renames the temple here in the abbot's honor. The abbot's name was Ch'ung-sun 重巽, whom Liu refers to as the "transcendent master." Liu often joined the abbot in his quarters in the temple's east wing reading texts—texts that would have been written on palm leaves in India but on paper or silk in China. I don't know what text Liu is quoting (or paraphrasing). Most likely it was something the abbot gave him to read. Ch'ung-sun was a student of both Zen and Tientai Buddhism. Liu's quarters were in the west wing. (1134)

III. The West Balcony of Yungchou's
Lunghsing Temple 永州龍興寺西軒記

At the beginning of the Yungchen period [805], I was labeled a partisan and forced to leave the Department of State Affairs. I was banished to Shaochou, but on the way there I was degraded further to be the assistant magistrate of Yungchou. When I arrived, I had no place to live, so I settled in the west wing of Lunghsing Temple. I had long been familiar with the teachings of Sakyamuni, and this was actually something I had hoped for. However, the room where I took shelter was quite dark. It was set in the shade, and the windows faced north. But since the temple was located above the town, and the west wing faced the current of a mighty river, and beyond the river to the west were forested mountains and valleys, I cut through the west wall and made a door, and beyond the door a balcony, so I could see everything beyond the treetops. Without having to move my mat or my desk I suddenly had a grand view.

That room is now a room of the past and that mat and desk are now a place of the past. When something that was dark becomes bright, does it not become a different thing? By realizing the Way of the Buddha, one can turn ignorant views into true knowledge and delusions into true awareness, thus exchanging darkness for light. Is this nature of ours any different? Anyone who can cut through my wall of ignorance, open up a door to spiritual light, and extend a balcony to welcome what lies beyond, I am their disciple. And so I am writing this down for two reasons: one is to record what is outside my door, the other is to have something to give Master Sun.

永貞年，余名在黨人，不容於尚書省。出為邵州，道　貶永州司馬。至則無以為居，居龍興寺西序之下。余知釋氏之道且久，固所願也。然余所庇之屋甚隱蔽，其戶北向，居昧昧也。寺之居於是州為高。西序之西，屬當大江之流，江之外，山谷林麓甚眾。於是鑿西墉以為戶，戶之外為軒，以臨羣木之杪，無不矚焉。不徙席，不運几，而得大觀。

　　夫室，嚮者之室也，席與几，嚮者之處也。嚮也昧而今也顯，豈異物耶。因悟夫佛之道，可以轉惑見為真智，即羣迷為正覺，捨大闇為光明。夫性豈異

物耶。孰能為余鑿大昏之墉，闢靈照之戶，廣應物之軒者，吾將與為徒。遂書為二，其一志諸戶外，其一以貽巽上人焉. (751)

11. Thirty Couplets on Fahua Temple's Stone Gate Hermitage 法華寺石門精室三十韻

I felt depressed and sick from worry
to ease my heart I needed lighter air
I had been thinking of eminent monks
looking at East Mountain night and day
happily the sky finally cleared
happily the green world was alive
I was joined by my favorite cousin
we were excited as we set out
we followed a stream farther and farther
then stone steps higher and higher
past creepers and vines toward a storied structure
lichen and moss half covered the name
dense woods rose in front and back
sheer walls on either side
a fortress appeared out of the gloom
its parapets looked out on the river
we felt cut off from the world
as if we had climbed to the sky
the buildings were surrounded by cliffs
wherever we turned things changed

拘情病幽鬱，曠志寄高爽。願言懷名緇，東峰旦夕仰。
始欣雲雨霽，尤悅草木長。道同有愛弟，披拂恣心賞。
松谿窈窱入，石棧夤緣上。蘿葛綿層蘙，莓苔侵標牓。
密林互對聳，絕壁儼雙敞。潭崎出蒙籠，墟嶮臨滉瀁。
稍疑地脈斷，悠若天梯往。結構罩群崖，迴環驅萬象。

a kalpa seemed but the blink of an eye
the universe was there in our hands
emptiness and the source of all things
we saw our existence free of thoughts
free of the buzzing of gnats
and the fear of mountain spirits

how could we work for mere trifles
how could we bend at the waist
gazing at this most wondrous of sights
listening to the subtlest of sounds
today we finally understood
as never before we felt awake
if we don't continue this journey
how shall we live out this life
taking an uncommon path is rare
but we've never trusted empty names
getting free requires help from outside
bowing in silence and looking within
reflecting and respecting old ways
we've finally found our true clan

小劫不逾瞬，大千若在掌。體空得化元，觀有遺細想。
喧煩困蟻蠓，跼蹐疲魍魎。寸進諒何營，尋直非所枉。
探奇極遙矚，窮妙閱清響。理會方在今，神開庶殊曩。
茲游苟不嗣，浩氣竟誰養。道異誠所希，名賓匪余仗。
超攄藉外獎，倪默有內朗。鑑爾揖古風，終焉乃吾黨。

free of restraints living in seclusion
up high above the world of dust
ambition is a waste of effort
how could we follow the footprints of others
we lingered until the sun went down
looking into the distance entranced
at columns of geese in the fading light
wave upon wave of ever-changing clouds
the wind dying down then rising
the road below leading into the distance
prisoners in a cangue fear a flood
exiles far from home hate the wind
people who lost their way used to sigh
here are two who slipped away
what good is pining for home
there's an ancient likeness of the Buddha here

up a half-hidden trail not a foot wide
in an empty ten-foot-square cell
hearing profound words worth repeating
we bowed our heads until dawn

潛軀委韁鎖，高步謝塵垗。蓄志徒為勞，追蹤將焉倣。
淹留值頹暮，眷戀睎遐壤。映日雁聯軒，翻雲波泱漭。
殊風紛已萃，鄉路悠且廣。羈木畏漂浮，離旌倦搖蕩。
昔人歎違志，出處今已兩。何用期所歸，浮圖有遺像。
幽蹊不盈尺，虛室有函丈。微言信可傳，申旦稽吾顙。

....

NOTE: Written in Yungchou in the early summer of 806. Fahua Temple (now called Kaoshan 高山) was just below the summit of East Mountain (Tung-shan 東山) and less than a kilometer north of Liu's residence at Lunghsing Temple. Stone Gate Hermitage was at the southern end of the grounds of Fahua. Liu first visited this hermitage with the town's magistrate Feng Hsu 馮 敘 in the third month. This poem recounts a subsequent visit with his cousin Liu Tsung-chih. The temple and its hermitage became one of Liu's favorite haunts. The language makes what today would be a thirty-minute hike sound daunting. But for Liu, the bureaucrat, this was something new and wonderful and worthy of his skill with words. The phrase "ten-foot-square cell" refers to the abbot's room as well as to the abbot, in this case Chueh-chao 覺照, with whom Liu became close friends. (1187)

12. Building West Pavilion at Fahua Temple
構法華寺西亭

Banished to the far south of Ch'u
to a world full of hardships and dangers
I hiked to the loftiest temple
to relax and to do something fun
to the west dropped precipitous cliffs
as if they were spying on the town
but they were in a hard-to-reach valley
I couldn't get past the creepers and thorns
I told my attendants to use machetes
and to build a pavilion where the mountain fell away
dividing the pure and mundane
it looked like it was floating in the clouds
in the distance was a gathering of peaks
and eddies of clear water in the river below
as the sun went down past the railing
flocks of birds came back to roost
lotuses overflowed with color
bamboos were streaked with tears
I felt like I had removed my shackles
my cares disappeared and my heart felt at peace
I've been distressed since I was exiled
today I could finally smile
but happiness rarely lasts long
thoughts of separation entangled me again
looking north toward those I love
then toward the hill tribes to the south
I'm putting this aside and not speaking of it again
let me just enjoy this moment

竄身楚南極，山水窮險艱。步登最高寺，蕭散任疎頑。
西垂下斗絕，欲似窺人寰。反如在幽谷，榛翳不可攀。
命童恣披翦，茸宇橫斷山。割如判清濁，飄若昇雲間。
遠岫攢衆頂，澄江抱清灣。夕照臨軒墮，棲鳥當我還。
菡萏溢嘉色，篔簹遺清斑。神舒屏羈鎖，志適忘幽屏。
棄逐久枯槁，迨今始開顏。賞心難久留，離念來相關。
北望間親愛，南瞻雜夷蠻。置之勿復道，且寄須臾閑。

....

NOTE: Written in Yungchou in the summer of 806. While Liu was still living at Lunghsing Temple, he donated part of his salary to build a pavilion at this temple on the west-facing slope of East Mountain. The brown streaks on the bamboo in this region are said to be the tears of the two Ladies of the Hsiang 湘妃 who drowned themselves in the river's waters when they heard their husband, Emperor Shun, had died. (1196)

IV. On Building West Pavilion at Yungchou's Fahua Temple 永州法華寺新作西亭記

Fahua Temple is located at the highest spot in Yungchou. The abbot is named Chueh-chao, and he lives along the temple's west veranda. Beyond the veranda there's a forest of bamboo, and beyond that the mountain drops off. The mass of different kinds of bamboo formed an impenetrable screen, and I thought that if I cleared it away there would be a grand view. Master Chao said, "There's a pond of lotuses down below, and the view extends across the Hsiang to the mountains. If you actually manage to clear everything away, you should be able to see quite far." Accordingly, I told my attendants to grab some axes and machetes and to cut everything down. Once all the vegetation was cleared away, a host of sights appeared. Vast and limitless, the sky seemed higher, and the land wider. The height of the hills and mountains and the size of the rivers and marshes all seemed to have grown and expanded. The wonder of this place was something I couldn't keep from passing on to those to come. Since I was rusticated to this prefecture as its assistant magistrate and was an official with no office, I could do what I pleased. So I used my salary to build this pavilion, making it 20 feet high and the same on each side.

Someone wondered why Master Chao hadn't done this earlier, since he already lived here. I replied that the sages of the past didn't have to rise from their meditation cushions to see the reality of form and emptiness, or to wander between the beginning and end of things. Their light transcended nirvana, and their awareness transcended existence. That being so, could what had previously been an obstruction really have been an obstruction? And could what has now become an opening really be an opening? How do we know he whom we call Light of Awareness didn't already realize this? Is it not we in our concern about what is open or obstructed, about what exists or doesn't, who restrict ourselves? Someone said, "That being so, why not write this down?" And so, I've written it on a rock.

法華寺居永州，地最高。有僧曰覺照，照居寺西廡下，廡之外有大竹數萬，又其外山形下絕。然而薪蒸篠簜蒙雜擁蔽，吾意伐而除之，必將有見焉。照謂余曰是其下有陂池芙蕖，申以湘水之流，眾山之會。果去是，其見遠矣。遂命僕人持刀斧，羣而翦焉。叢莽下頹，萬類皆出。曠焉茫焉，天為之益高，地為之加闢。丘陵山谷之峻，江湖池澤之大，咸若有增廣之者。夫其地之奇，必以遺乎後，不可曠也。余時謫為州司馬，官外乎常員，而心得無事。乃取官之祿秩，以為其亭，其高且廣，蓋方丈者二焉。

或異照之居於斯，而不蚤為是也。余謂昔之上人者，不起宴坐，足以觀於空色之實，而游乎物之終始。其照也逾寂，其覺也逾有。然則嚮之礙之者為果礙耶。今之闢之者為果闢耶。彼所謂覺而照者，吾詎知其不由是道也。豈若吾族之挈挈於通塞有無之方以自狹耶。或曰然則宜書之。乃書於石。

....

NOTE: Written in Yungchou in 806. The abbot's name means "light of awareness." Paper money was already in use at this time, but prices were still stated in the number of coins. Liu's monthly salary would have been around 3,000, assuming he received the standard amount for his position as a sixth-grade official. The cost of building such a structure wouldn't have been more than a few hundred. (749)

13. Climbing West Tower on an Oppressively Hot Summer Night 夏夜苦熱登西樓

The heat was so oppressive I got up at midnight
I climbed the stairs in my underwear
the summer air hung above the hills and marshes
light flickered in the depths of the river of stars
the daily fireball had burned up the dew
the countryside was quiet and the wind had died
from a barrel I ladled out warm water
then I opened the door to the furnace
I lingered outside at the railing
dripping more sweat than I could wipe away
don't tell me about the detoxifying benefits
I looked up and appealed to the stars of the Dipper
excuse me for not being from Kushe
staying that still is beyond me

苦熱中夜起，登樓獨褰衣。山澤凝暑氣，星漢湛光輝。
火晶燥露滋，野靜停風威。探湯汲陰井，煬竈開重扉。
憑欄久徬徨，流汗不可揮。莫辯亭毒意，仰訴璿與璣。
諒非姑射子，靜勝安能希。

....

Note: Written in Yungchou in the summer of 806. This would have been Liu's first experience with such heat and humidity since traveling with his father as a boy. "West Tower" most likely refers to Lunghsing Temple's drum tower. Most Buddhist temples had two towers for announcing the beginning and end of the monastic day, with the drum tower just inside and to the left of the entrance and the bell tower to the right. The gate and buildings of Lunghsing Temple faced south. The "river of stars" refers to the Milky Way. The ancient Chinese believed the Big Dipper bestows rain and moisture. In the first chapter of *Chuangtzu*, Master Chuang says, "There's a man with spiritual powers on Mount Kushe whose skin is like ice… who never gets hot, even when the earth burns." According to Lao-tzu's *Taoteching* (45), "Stillness overcomes heat." (1197)

14–18. Five Odes to Master Sun's Temple 巽公院五詠

One: The Pure Land Hall 淨土堂

Bound by attachments without beginning
drowning in a sea of endless suffering
reaching this life on the round of rebirth
we've entered the triple gate of emptiness at last
a pure world appears in this painted hall
a dozen brightly colored statues and murals
the fragrance of the purest incense
and the subtle songs of the Dharma
bowing in humility before our teacher
we leave the dust and darkness behind

結習自無始，淪溺窮苦源。流形及茲世，始悟三空門。
華堂開淨域，圖像煥且繁。清泠焚衆香，微妙歌法音。
稽首媿導師，超遙謝塵昏。

Two: The Lecture Hall 曲講堂

Cessation doesn't mean extinction
how can we get free of language
this is why this lecture hall was built
there's a bodhisattva inside
the sage's silence is expressed in words
but distinctions don't mean knowledge
choose the path between emptiness and illusion
who are you looking for in name and form
try to let go of what you hear
forget ideas when you think

寂滅本非斷，文字安可離。曲堂何為設，高士方在斯。
聖默寄言宣，分別乃無知。趣中即空假，名相與誰期。
願言絕聞得，忘意聊思惟。

Three: The Meditation Hall 禪堂

It begins with the weaving of thatch
surrounding a vacant space
wildflowers fall beyond a darkened door
inside is someone without schemes
entering existence without grabbing hold
looking at emptiness without analyzing
ten thousand sounds arise from conditions
deep within there's stillness in noise
the mind and the world are essentially alike
birds leave no tracks when they fly

發地結菁茆，團團抱虛白。山花落幽戶，中有忘機客。
涉有本非取，照空不待析。萬籟俱緣生，窅然喧中寂。
心境本同如，鳥飛無遺跡。

Four: Lotus Pavilion 芙蓉亭

The new pavilion rests on red pillars
beyond the painted wood are lotuses in bloom
the morning breeze spreads their subtle scent
the icy dew drenches their lustrous petals
rising detached from the world
each blossom utterly unique
we keep hearing about form and emptiness
but who created material things
the lingering quiet of the autumn moon
the distant sound of a temple bell

新亭俯朱檻，嘉木開芙蓉。清香晨風遠，溽彩寒露濃。
瀟洒出人世，低昂多異容。嘗聞色空喻，造物誰為工。
留連秋月晏，迢遞來山鍾。

Five: Bitter Bamboo Bridge 苦竹橋

This perilous bridge is on a less-traveled trail
one that winds through scattered bamboo
their dry sheaths revealing unbreakable joints
their thin bark encasing hollow hearts
I looked down at the rippling stream
and listened to the rustling above
the setting sun was flickering through the mist
wild birds were calling across the mountain
this might not be the main way up
but it's shady and a good place to rest

危橋屬幽徑，繚繞穿疏林。迸籜分苦節，輕篠抱虛心。
俯瞰涓涓流，仰聆蕭蕭吟。差池下煙日，嘲哳鳴山禽。
諒無要津用，棲息有餘陰。

. . . .

NOTE: Written in Yungchou in the late summer or early fall of 806, the time of year when lotuses are in bloom, shade is welcome, and the autumn moon announces cooler weather is on the way. This set of poems was written at and about Lunghsing Temple and its environs.

ONE: Liu financed the renovation of the temple's Pure Land Hall shortly after his mother died in the sixth month of 806. Ceremonies in such halls focused on the rebirth of devotees in the Pure Land of Amitabha Buddha. The "triple gate of emptiness" is the teaching that all things are empty of self-existence, form, and anything desirable. Pure Land Buddhism's *Visualization of Paradise Sutra* 觀無量壽佛經 describes in detail the meditations whereby that land is made manifest and was often used by artists to cover shrine halls and cave walls with two-dimensional depictions.

TWO: The term "cessation" is commonly used by Buddhists for "nirvana." In addition to Zen, the temple's abbot taught Tientai Buddhism, which emphasizes the middle path between emptiness and illusion. "Name and form" refer to the world as we imagine it and the world as we perceive it, the world inside us and the world outside us, which are the result of our imagination and projections.

Four: Liu also financed construction of this pavilion. He liked to have a place outside where he could sit and drink with friends. The inseparable nature of form (*rupa:* our external world) and emptiness (*shunyata:* the absence of self-existence) is one of the central teachings of Mahayana Buddhism, as in the *Heart Sutra* 心經: "Form is emptiness and emptiness is form / form is not separate from emptiness and emptiness is not separate from form / whatever is form is emptiness and whatever is emptiness is form."

Five: The title and the third line of this poem involve a play on the word *k'u* 苦 (bitter, enduring). In the title it refers to a variety of bamboo that is too bitter to eat but useful for construction. In the third line, its appearance in the term *k'u-chieh* 苦節 (bitter/enduring-joints) is interpreted as the ability to maintain one's integrity in the face of hardship. This bridge wouldn't have been far from the temple and was probably the one mentioned in Liu's later account of his landscaping project on the slope north of the temple grounds, which he recounts in prose piece XIX. (1234)

V. Restoring the Pure Land Hall at Yungchou's Lunghsing Temple 永州龍興寺修淨土院記

Over ten thousand *li* west of the Central Plains is a country called India. This is where the tathagata Sakyamuni appeared. He once said that a million buddha lands to the west is a world known as Paradise and a buddha named Amitabha Tathagata. Within that realm the three evils and eight afflictions don't exist, it's adorned by every kind of jewel, its inhabitants are free from the ten bondages and nine distresses, and bodhisattvas are among their friends. If a person can make a great vow with the utmost sincerity to be reborn there, and if their power of concentration is sufficient, they will be reborn in that land and finally dwell beyond the Three Realms. As long as they do not turn away from the path of the buddhas, they will not be disappointed in their words. During the Chin dynasty, Master Hui-yuan of Lushan composed "The Samadhi of Reciting the Name of the Buddha," which was a great encouragement to those of that age. Later, Master Yi of Tientai wrote his "Treatise Concerning Ten Doubts about the Pure Land," which spread this teaching far and wide. It was complete and succinct and wonderfully subtle, and all those who had previously been confused came to rely on it. Thus, he left behind something rare that surpassed the work of others.

Li Ch'eng-chih, an earlier magistrate of Yungchou, and the monk Fa-lin established a Pure Land hall in the eastern grounds of Lung–hsing Temple and often conducted ceremonies there. That was over twenty years ago, and the hall was starting to fall apart, and the murals and statues were beginning to fade and crumble. Master Sun now lives there, and he began to restore it. The Master cultivates the Supreme Vehicle and understands its truths. Following the invisible footsteps of emptiness instead of form, he has reached the true source. And understanding how to use the language of existence and nonexistence, he has entered the realm of reality, where the world and wisdom are one, where practice and reason merge. Thus, despite having the goal of being reborn in that land, he hasn't renounced appearances or skillful means and has resolved to restore this place for the use of future practitioners. The faithful have repaired the murals and buddha statues, and all the ceremonial paraphernalia is complete. The current magistrate, Feng Hsu, built a huge gate as an indication of its status, and I expanded the drainage and built a veranda on all four sides and finished things by adding canopies and flags to the statues of the Two Guardians. Indeed, those who are able to seek that birth which is beyond birth should know that the raft to carry them there is here. I then wrote the text of the Tientai "Treatise Concerning Ten Doubts" on one of the walls to inspire the faith of those who see it.

中州之西數萬里，有國曰身毒。釋迦牟尼如來示現之地。彼佛言曰西方過十萬億佛土，有世界曰極樂，佛號無量壽如來。其國無有三惡八難，眾寶以為飾，其人無有十纏九惱，羣聖以為友。有能誠心大願，歸心是土者，苟念力具足，則往生彼國，然後出三界之外。其於佛道無退轉者，其言無所欺也。晉時廬山遠法師作念佛三昧詠，大勸于時。其後天台顗大師著釋淨土十疑論，弘宣其教。周密微妙，迷者咸賴焉。蓋其留異跡而去者甚眾。

永州龍興寺，前刺史李承晊及僧法林，置淨土堂于寺之東偏，常奉斯事。逮今餘二十年，廉隅毀頓，圖像崩墜。會異上人居其宇下，始復理焉。上人者，修最上乘，解第一義。無體空折色之跡，而造乎真源，通假有借無之名，而入於實相。境與智合，事與理并。故雖往生之因，亦相用不捨，誓葺茲宇，以開後學。有信士圖為佛像，法相甚具焉。今刺史馮公作大門以表其位，余遂周延四阿，環以廊廡，續二大士之像，繪蓋幢幡，以成就之。嗚呼，有能求無生之生者，知舟筏之存乎是。遂以天台十疑論書于牆宇，使觀者起信焉。

....

NOTE: Written in Yungchou in 806. The Three Realms, which include all possible forms of existence, are those of Desire, Form, and Formlessness. The founder of the Pure Land school in China was Hui-yuan 慧遠, who conducted the first Pure Land ceremonies at the foot of Lushan 廬山 in 402. The "Treatise Concerning Ten Doubts" was composed around 590 by Chih-yi 智顗, the founder of the Tientai school of Buddhism. The Supreme Vehicle refers to the Mahayana, and the Two Guardians are Heng 哼 and Ha 哈, two Chou-dynasty generals who became elevated to the status of door gods and, later, protectors of the Dharma. (754)

19. Climbing the Boulders on Puchou Island and Looking Across at the River's Mouth and in the Distance at Tantao Island Opposite Hsiangling Rock 登蒲洲石磯望橫江口潭島深迴斜對香零山

All night I was beset by worries
when the fog cleared I went down to the ford
the gibbon howls had tapered off
I climbed the rocks to view the river
at sunup the island was quiet
the shore's flawless sand was bright
the sun illuminated the birds above
and shimmered on the fish below
where the two rivers met and turned west
I marveled at the jewel of this land
its lone peak leaning northward
its cool forest home to spirits
the current here frightens people
the island appears to be moving
people were digging clay
cutting reeds and catching fish
a lovely sight but no relief
my mind was on a distant journey
I need to get free of this bondage
the depression I feel needs to end
I went back to my old room singing
but deceiving myself is no fun

隱憂倦永夜，凌霧臨江津。猿鳴稍已疏，登石娛清淪。
日出洲渚靜，澄明晶無垠。浮暉翻高禽，沉景照文鱗。
雙江匯西奔，詭怪潛坤珍。孤山乃北峙，森爽棲靈神。
洄潭或動容，島嶼疑搖振。陶埴茲擇土，蒲魚相與鄰。
信美非所安，羈心屢逡巡。糾結良可解，紆鬱亦已伸。
高歌返故室，自誷非所欣。

NOTE: Written in Yungchou in 806. The title says this was written on Puchou Island 蒲洲, also known as Pingchou 萍州 or Pintao 頻島 Island, which is located on the west shore of the Hsiao where it is joined by the Hsiang. But in the title, Liu says the river's mouth was on the opposite shore and he could see Tanchou Island and Hsiangling Mountain from where he was standing. The problem with this is that Tanchou Island and Hsiangling Mountain are 10 kilometers south of Puchou Island and around the river's next upstream bend. Hence, they would not have been visible on the clearest of days. Calling Hsiangling a mountain is likewise poetic exaggeration. It is only 20 meters high and no more than that across. During winter it's usually connected to the west shore, but in summer it's in midstream. Tanchou is an even smaller outcrop of sand and rocks nearby but in midstream. Another problem is that where the Hsiao and Hsiang meet, their combined waters flow northeast, not west. The only solution I can think of is that Liu was standing on the boulders along the east shore of the Hsiao at the ford south of town, and while looking at Hsiangling "Mountain" in the river he mistook the merging multiple mouths of Rock Creek 石澗 at Hundred Family Shoals 百家瀨 on the west shore for the waters of the Hsiang—see prose pieces XII and XIV. At that point the combined waters do, indeed, flow west, before turning north. If the date of 806 is accurate, perhaps that would explain the inconsistencies, as Liu was newly arrived. (1191)

20. Twenty Couplets on Visiting Chaoyang Cliff and Climbing to West Pavilion

遊朝陽巖遂登西亭二十韻

Exile is different from seclusion
there's hiking but not far from town
I was hoping to lighten my depression
not to imitate Po-yi or Ch'ao-fu
from the cliff I looked down on the river
a dragon was lurking in a cave
sunlight spread across the landscape
and gathered around the tops of the trees
at the summit rose West Pavilion
beyond the roof I looked out into space
behind me was where the constellations rose
below was where the clouds and rain formed
but this wasn't my home
that would be the shade of green thatch
as a boy I traveled the great rivers
as an official I crossed the Han and Hsiao passes
the family farm was on the banks of the Feng
half an acre of flat fertile soil
terraces and buildings covered a hill
there were ponds and irrigation canals

謫棄殊隱淪，登陟非遠郊。所懷緩伊鬱，詎欲肩夷巢。
高巖瞰清江，幽窟潛神蛟。開曠延陽景，迴薄攢林梢。
西亭構其巔，反宇臨呀庨。背瞻星辰興，下見雲雨交。
惜非吾鄉土，得以蔭菁茆。羈貫去江介，世仕尚函崤。
故墅即澧川，數畝均肥磽。臺館集荒丘，池塘疏沉坳。

but attachment to pomp and regalia
led to complaints from the more austere
weak willed and truly without talent
I put too much stock in mere trifles
my exile was certainly deserved

I've already accepted my shame
I planted artemisia and fleabane in the courtyard
spiderwebs now cover my windows
I look forward to the visits of travelers
in their narrow-hulled boats with long useless oars
I offer them water as opposed to wine
I gather wild plants for a treat
we talk at length about the Tao
I entertain without flutes or strings
this life of leisure keeps cares away
such simple ways dispel noise
roosters don't fail me at dawn
I listen to them crow in the wind or rain
hoping for more of these long idle days
I brought my kitchen here with me

會有圭組戀，遂貽山林嘲。薄軀信無庸，瑣屑劇斗筲。
囚居固其宜，厚羞久已包。庭除植蓬艾，隙牖懸蟏蛸。
所賴山水客，扁舟枉長梢。揖流敵清觴，掇野代嘉肴。
適道有高言，取樂非絃匏。逍遙屏幽昧，澹薄辭喧啾。
晨雞不余欺，風雨聞嘐嘐。再期永日閑，提挈移中庖。

....

NOTE: Written in Yungchou in the ninth month of 806. Chaoyang Cliff is on the west shore of the Hsiao across the river from Lunghsing Temple. West Pavilion (not the pavilion of the same name Liu built at Fahua Temple) was a thatched structure built at the top of the cliff by the poet Yuan Chieh 元結 forty years earlier. Po-yi 伯夷 and Ch'ao-fu 巢父 were hermits who lived in the second and third millennia BC, respectively. On the Hsiao and Hsiang Rivers, boats relied on trackers to pull them upstream—hence the uselessness of oars. Going downriver was another story. Liu, of course, was not free of cares. He thinks back to living with his mother and sisters along the Feng when he was a boy and traveling with his father along the Yangtze. The reference to the passes puzzled me at first, as prior to his exile the only time Liu visited Hanku Pass was when his father was serving in Lingpao and he was ten. But then I realized he was technically an official when he was exiled and would have revisited Hanku Pass on his way to Yungchou. The mention of Hsiaokuan

Pass as well suggests that this was the route he took on the same journey: east from Ch'ang-an and through Hanku Pass then south through Hsiaokuan Pass "as an official." In any case, despite all these memories, here he is writing a poem about visiting the pavilion across the river, and he can't help thinking about his quarters at Lunghsing Temple. Whatever his memories involved, he decided he was going to be there long enough to plant some herbs and that he may as well cook something other than what the monks ate. (1189)

21–22. LAMENT: TWO POEMS 感遇二首

ONE

Cold air stirs in the west
in the North Woods the crows sound alarmed
they can't change where they live
or roost on leafless trees
the swan is gone and not coming back
the road to Wu was long and hard
it's useless to sigh about current excesses
dropping copper balls on drums for the sound
the East Sea has always been stormy
but the South Wind too is wild
the moment the sky turns dark
stars worry about the moon
people are addicted to money and sex
they amass possessions at any price
as soon as a tree stands out
sharp axes seek it out
I throw on a robe at midnight
and soak the sleeves with tears
walking on the year's first frost
who thinks about the coming cold

西陸動涼氣，驚烏號北林。栖息豈殊性，集枯安可任。
鴻鵠去不返，勾吳阻且深。徒嗟日沉湎，丸鼓騖奇音。
東海久搖蕩，南風已駿駿。坐使青天暮，小星愁太陰。
眾情嗜姦利，居貨損千金。危根一以振，齊斧來相尋。
攬衣中夜起，感物涕盈襟。微霜眾所踐，誰念歲寒心。

TWO

Dawn lights the winter wilds
crows rise up from the brambles
enjoying a good caw

they swarm the Western Hills
all day the wind swirls
leaves bury what plants remain
there's no safe place to roost
and hawks fill the sky

旭日照寒野，鴛斯起蒿萊。啁啾有餘樂，飛舞西陵隈。
迴風旦夕至，零葉委陳荄。所棲不足恃，鷹隼縱橫來。

....

NOTE: Written in Yungchou in the late fall of 806 and inspired by similar
poems by Juan Chi 阮籍 and Ch'en Tzu-ang 陳子昂 but especially by a set of
twelve poems with the same title written by Chang Chiu-ling 張九齡 follow-
ing his exile in 726. Thus, Liu sets both poems in Loyang, where the court
was located during Juan's and Ch'en's time and also during Chang's days as
prime minister.

ONE: This is a critique of the court's suppression of the reform faction to
which Liu belonged. The Chinese associate the seasons with the cardinal
directions and link autumn with the west. Here, too, this could refer to
Loyang's Western Hills, mentioned in the second poem. The North Woods
was the location of the court in Loyang. The swan refers to Wang Shu-wen,
leader of the reform faction of which Liu was a member. Wang was allowed
to commit suicide several months before this was written while mourning
the death of his mother at his home in the former state of Wu. Liu also sees
peaceful times as being over, the country unsettled, and the court engaging
in indulgences similar to those of Emperor Yuan 元帝 (r. 48–32 BC) of the
Han dynasty, whose pastimes included dropping copper balls on drums just
to hear the sound. The East Sea refers to the provinces along the northeastern
seaboard that had become more or less independent of central government
control following the An Lu-shan Rebellion (755–763). The South Wind nor-
mally refers to the policies of a benevolent ruler and is usually described as
"mild." Its description as "wild" here suggests instead the unwillingness of
regional governors in South China to acknowledge the authority of the court.
Meanwhile, Liu sees the officials at court worrying about anyone trying to
outshine or rise above their assembled ranks. As for the last line, Liu is sug-
gesting lesser officials are relieved that the heat of summer is over and are

unconcerned with the cold weather to come. Enduring hardships was a virtue praised by Confucius, who once said, "When the year turns cold, we know the pine and cypress will be the last to shed their needles" (*Analects* 論語 9.27).

Two: As in the first poem, the crows represent the reformers at court. Here the hawks represent their opponents. Loyang's Western Hills were the location of a number of graves belonging to pre-T'ang emperors, to whom Liu looks for guidance. (1255)

23–25. HARD ROADS: THREE POEMS 行路難三首

ONE

Don't you see
K'ua-fu chasing the sun and peering into the Abyss
jumping into the North Sea and over the Kunlun Mountains
breaking through the firmament and out into space
in the blink of an eye leaving the stars behind
suddenly exhausted dying of thirst on the roadside
foxes and wasps fighting over his remains
and dwarves in the North nine inches high
clapping and yelling making all kinds of noise
nibbling on seeds and sipping raindrops
living out their allotted years
making grandiose vows with little to show
wasting the love of their children

君不見
夸父逐日窺虞淵，跳踉北海超崑崙。披霄決漢出沆瀁，瞥裂左右遺星辰。
須臾力盡道渴死，狐鼠蜂蟻爭噬吞。北方踔人長九寸，開口抵掌更笑喧。
啾啾飲食滴與粒，生死亦足終天年。睢盱大志小成遂，坐使兒女相悲憐。

TWO

The court sends woodsmen into a thousand mountains
with orders to choose pillars and beams
in ancient groves they cut ten and keep one
shattering the axles of hundred-oxen teams
blocking roadways with piles of logs
leaving hills in ruins and mountains in flames
and nothing that remains intact
no creek or gorge survives the trampling
and most of the lumber isn't used
slopes are stripped and ridges left barren
then there's an armory or a palace fire

and builders look nervous expecting to be blamed
don't you see
the great trees of South Mountain becoming scarce
and those who care even scarcer

虞衡斤斧羅千山，工命採斫杙與椽。深林土剪十取一，百牛連靷摧雙轅。
萬圍千尋妨道路，東西蹶倒山火焚。遺餘毫末不見保，躑躅澗壑何當存。
群材未成質已夭，突兀砟豁空巖巒。柏梁天災武庫火，匠石狼顧相愁冤。
君不見
南山棟梁益稀少，愛材養育誰復論。

THREE

When snow blocks the roads and bridges turn to ice
nobles burn charcoal in homes of carved jade
dragons breathe flames and tigers growl
panthers and bears look ready to pounce
ridge upon ridge emits a red glow
clouds of every color waft rare perfumes
beauties light halls with their earrings
snowy mountains and valleys glitter in the dawn
the procession of stars doesn't stop
suddenly swallows build nests on painted beams
terraces and pavilions outside look bejeweled
and dead coals are forgotten like last night's sky
golden times end and the high become low
fancy mats and fans are no use then

飛雪斷道冰成梁，侯家燒炭雕玉房。蟠龍吐耀虎喙張，熊蹲豹躑爭低昂。
攢巒叢崿射朱光，丹霞翠霧飄奇香。美人四向迴明璫，雪山冰谷晞太陽。
星躔奔走不得止，奄忽雙燕棲虹梁。風臺露榭生光飾，死灰棄置參與商。
盛時一去貴反賤，桃笙葵扇安可當。

....

NOTE: Written in Yungchou in the winter of 806, while reflecting on life in Ch'ang-an. The title was used by poets to voice complaints, with the line "don't you see" often used to begin sections of such poems.

ONE: Liu likens himself to the mythical creature known as K'ua-fu, who tried to race the sun to where it slept at night but died of thirst on the way. The Kunlun Mountains marked the western edge of Chinese territory. Liu also compares members of court (in the North) to the smallest creatures, incapable of the tasks they boast of undertaking and undeserving of even their own children's love.

TWO: The Cedar Beam Fire in 104 BC burned a large part of the Han-dynasty palace, and the Armory Fire of 295 did the same to the royal arms depository during the Chin dynasty. The South Mountains refer to the Chungnan Mountains immediately south of Ch'ang-an. Many of China's sages have made these mountains their home. During the T'ang dynasty, some would-be officials went so far as to build huts there hoping to be noticed by the court.

THREE: For those who could afford such things, charcoal was carved into the shape of animals and mountains that formed a glowing wilderness when it burned. (1239)

26. Orange Trees Flourish in the South 南中榮橘柚

The orange possesses an unbending nature
destined for life in this fiery land
it illuminates whole groves with its red and green
its perfume lasts through year-end
north of the Huai a different wind blows
covering my hometown with snow
holding a branch why do I sigh
I see Mount Hsiung and Mount Hsiang to the north

橘柚懷貞質，受命此炎方。密林耀朱綠，晚歲有餘芳。
殊風限清漢，飛雪滯故鄉。攀條何所歎，北望熊與湘。

. . . .

NOTE: Written in Yungchou in the winter of 806. Identifying with the orange, Liu blames his exile on his "unbending nature." The Huai River (called the Chinghan here in the Chinese) marks the limit of regular oranges. North of the Huai, oranges all have much thicker skins. Mount Hsiung (or Hsiung-er) is 100 kilometers west of Loyang and marked the dividing line between the Yellow River and Yangtze watersheds. Mount Hsiang (elsewhere called Chunshan 君山) is a small island in the middle of Tungting Lake, into which the waters of the Hsiang empty before joining the Yangtze. It was often used to refer to South China (South China of the T'ang). Liu finds himself not only south of the North, but south of the South. The title is taken from "In Reply to Wang Chin-an" 酬王晉安 by Hsieh T'iao 謝朓: "Orange trees flourish in the south / how could you know where wild geese fly" 南中榮橘柚，寧知鴻雁飛. Liu later planted hundreds of orange trees in Yungchou and also in Liuchou (see poem 136). (1233)

27. Early Spring in Lingling 零陵早春

Before it departed I asked Spring
when it would reach the Ch'in Plains
and could it carry a dream back home
all the way to my old garden

問春從此去，幾日到秦原。憑寄還鄉夢，殷懃入故園。

....

Note: Written in Yungchou in the spring of 807 while Liu was living at Lunghsing Temple. Lingling was another name for Yungchou and is still used for the old city. The city now called Yungchou is 25 kilometers to the north. The Ch'in Plains refer to the area once occupied by the ancient state of Ch'in, which unified China for the first time in 255 BC and established its capital across the river from where Ch'ang-an was later built. Liu's last place of residence in the capital was just outside the main gate of the Forbidden City. But here he is thinking of the farm he lived on as a boy, with his mother and sisters, southwest of the capital on the Feng River. (1237)

28. Receiving a Present of New Tea Picked by Master Sun among the Bamboo, I Offer a Poem in Thanks 巽上人以竹間自採新茶見贈酬之以詩

From fragrant bushes shaded by Hsiang bamboo
drenched with the purest dew
once again this Himalayan visitor
gathered their magic buds at dawn
beside a mist-shrouded rocky stream
next to a soaring red cliff
in a basket of artful shape and color
jade of the most perfect kind
I told the boy to heat the good stove
the scent reached dark and distant places
washing away cares it revealed my true face
ridding me of faults it led me to the source
not unlike that bowl of sweet dew
the Buddha once used to perfume Vaisali
this companion of immortals leaves me speechless
with something more precious than sunset-red wine

芳叢翳湘竹，零露凝清華。復此雪山客，晨朝掇靈芽。
蒸煙俯石瀨，咫尺凌丹崖。圓方麗奇色，圭璧無纖瑕。
呼兒爨金鼎，餘馥延幽遐。滌慮發真照，還源蕩昏邪。
猶同甘露飯，佛事薰毗耶。咄此蓬瀛侶，無乃貴流霞。

....

NOTE: Written in Yungchou, most likely in the spring of 807. Master Sun refers to Ch'ung-sun, the abbot of Lunghsing Temple. Tea is usually picked early in the morning, with the first pick of the year typically occurring in late March. The bamboo named for the Hsiang River is a mottled variety, with brown splotches on green canes. The foothills of the Himalayas (Snowy Mountains) were where the Buddha lived at the beginning of his spiritual career. Here, Master Sun takes his place. The Buddha once sent a bowl of dew-scented rice to the layman Vimalakirti, who was lying ill in the city of Vaisali and whose place is taken here by Liu. The term "sweet dew" refers to moisture gathered before it reaches the ground. It also refers to the saliva produced from the roof of the mouth during meditation. Every once in a while, we realize a poet in ancient China was rarely alone. If not accompanied by one or more friends, there was almost always an attendant or two carrying a zither or tea paraphernalia. Taoist immortals brewed an alcoholic beverage that looked like and made one feel like the rose-colored clouds of sunset. If I come across the recipe, I'll put it in the next edition. (1136)

29. For the Elder from Chianghua 贈江華長老

An old monk familiar with the workings of the Way
his voice is silent even his thoughts are still
after leaving Chungling last year
he followed the current and ended up here
inside a bare cell without an attendant
he hangs his clothes on the wall
he doesn't eat more than one meal
he sits cross-legged all night
a stand of bamboo creaks outside his window
a weathered pine drips above the well
wherever he happens to stay
the courtyard is filled with sweet-scented plants

老僧道機熟，默語心皆寂。去歲別春陵，沿流此投跡。
室空無侍者，巾屨唯掛壁。一飯不願餘，跏趺便終夕。
風窗疏竹響，露井寒松滴。偶地即安居，滿庭芳草積。

....

NOTE: Written in Yungchou in 807 at Lunghsing Temple. This monk followed
the Hsiao River downstream from Chianghua (aka Chungling), nowadays
known as Taochou. Yungchou was 75 kilometers to the north. Most senior
monks, or those who were more or less permanent residents of a monastery,
had an attendant—often children of families too poor to care for them. Lay-
men and visiting monks lived in the western, downhill, section of Lunghsing
and drew water from a well in the monastery courtyard. This monk's cell is
so bare, there's no closet for his clothes. (1135)

30. In Praise of the Past 詠史

In Yen there was a terrace of gold
it brought the Grand Guardian from afar
keeping silent when he was wronged
he accomplished great things in three years
he focused on expanding the frontiers
his influence spread to the sea
who could have known conditions would change
his own possessions would be lost
he paid no attention to gold or jewels
much less to the swarms of bugs
as rumors gave rise to plots
resentments and accusations multiplied
why didn't he plan for this sooner
he wasn't known for self-interest
concerning loyalty and public service
Master Yen too had something to say

燕有黃金臺，遠致望諸君。嘐嘐事強怨，三歲有奇勳。
悠哉闢疆理，東海漫浮雲。寧知世情異，嘉穀坐熇焚。
致令委金石，誰顧蠢蠕群。風波歘潛構，遺恨意紛紜。
豈不善圖後，交私非所聞。為忠不內顧，晏子亦垂文。

....

NOTE: Written in Yungchou in 807. Terms of exile were reconsidered after two years, and again after five. In Liu's case, it had been two years, and he was hoping loyalty and honesty would once more be in vogue among officials at court. In the first millennium BC, the king of the state of Yen constructed a terrace and covered it with gold, hoping the offer of wealth for the taking would attract worthy officials (*sic*) from other states. One such official was Yueh Yi 樂毅 (ca. 280 BC). Over the course of several years, Yueh became the king's chief general and carried out a series of successful campaigns against neighboring states, especially the state of Ch'i to the east. Despite his initial success, he was met with suspicion and accusations and was eventually forced to flee to his home state of Chao, where he was enfeoffed as the Grand

Guardian. Master Yen Ying 晏嬰 (578–500 BC), mentioned in the last line, was a prime minister who served the rulers of Ch'i several centuries before Yueh Yi's time. He was known for humility and honesty and praised similar qualities in the men whose deeds he recorded in his famous *Spring and Autumn Annals of Master Yen* 晏子春秋. (1257)

31. DRINKING WINE 飲酒

Feeling less than happy this morning
I got up and opened a fresh jug
lifting my cup I thanked the wine gods
for this gift to chase away cares
a moment later I felt different
suddenly the whole world was fine
the gloom disappeared from the mountains
the warmth of the sky filled the river
at the town's overgrown South Rampart
trees formed a canopy of leaves
the cool shade provided welcome relief
we heard some fine words here last night
once we were drunk we stopped talking
we stretched out on sweet-smelling grass
the wealthiest men in the past
surely possessed nothing like this

今旦少愉樂，起坐開清樽。舉觴酹先酒，遺我驅憂煩。
須臾心自殊，頓覺天地暄。連山變幽晦，綠水函晏溫。
藹藹南郭門，樹木一何繁。清陰可自庇，竟夕聞佳言。
盡醉無復辭，偃臥有芳蓀。彼哉晉楚富，此道未必存。

....

NOTE: Written in Yungchou in the summer of 807 shortly after Emperor
Hsien-tsung announced that the "appointments" of the eight men he ban-
ished two years earlier would continue for another three years. So much for
returning to court. Yungchou's South Rampart overlooked a bend of the
Hsiao River. It was half a kilometer beyond the town's South Gate and over a
kilometer from Liu's residence at Lunghsing Temple. (1253)

32. Transplanting a Hibiscus from the Shore of the Hsiang to My Lunghsing Hermitage
湘岸移木芙蓉植龍興精舍

With a loveliness that can't be hidden
how did this lone plant survive
flourishing on the Hsiang's west shore
plagued by wind and dew in fall
this beauty has since left the chilly water
its flowery profusion now graces my veranda
lotuses can hardly compare
up here on higher ground

有美不自蔽，安能守孤根。盈盈湘西岸，秋至風露繁。
麗影別寒水，穠芳委前軒。芰荷諒難雜，反此生高原。

....

NOTE: Written in Yungchou in the summer of 807, or perhaps the following summer, while Liu was residing at Lunghsing Temple. For the veranda, see prose piece III. The Hsiao River flows through Yungchou (Lingling) and is joined by the Hsiang just north of town. The Hsiang, though, is the more famous of the two rivers. Hence, Liu often uses its name when referring to the Hsiao, as he does here. The hibiscus can't survive winters north of the Yangtze. Liu's first encounter with the flower would have been when he was a boy traveling with his father south of the Yangtze. (1232)

33. River Snow 江雪

A thousand mountains and not a bird flying
ten thousand paths and not a single footprint
an old man in his raincoat in a solitary boat
fishes alone in the freezing river snow

千山鳥飛絕，萬逕人蹤滅。孤舟簑笠翁，獨釣寒江雪。

....

NOTE: Written in Yungchou in the winter of 807. The Yungchou region experienced a rare and an unusually heavy snowfall that year. Until modern times, the most common foul-weather gear in China for those who worked out of doors was made from the bark of palm trees. This is Liu's most famous poem. It's become a staple of painters. (1221)

34. Written in Jest about Old Stonegate, Tung-hsuan 戲題石門長老東軒

Old Stonegate's life is a dream
the grove of sandalwood trees was his doing
the person chanting isn't who he was
who is he chanting the *Lotus Sutra* for
seventy now he's forgotten how to scheme
concerning lust and love he's become too frail
don't go to East Veranda to view the scenes of spring
when flowers bloom at dawn that's when pheasants fly

石門長老身如夢，旃檀成林手所種。坐來念念非昔人，萬徧蓮花為誰用。
如今七十自忘機，貪愛都忘筋力微。莫向東軒春野望，花開日出雉皆飛。

....

Note: Written in Yungchou in the spring of 808 or 809. This monk's name, Tung-hsuan, means "east veranda," which Liu turns into a joke in the penultimate line. Shihmen, or Stonegate Hermitage, was just beyond the south gate of Fahua Monastery. This was where the monk Tung-hsuan lived. Apparently Tung-hsuan also planted some sandalwood trees while he was there. The *Lotus Sutra* is still a favorite among East Asian Buddhists, who chant such texts in part to accrue merit. Liu wonders for whom such merit is accrued if the self is an illusion and all that the chanter would achieve is no more than a dream. In the end, Liu sees his own life and that of his friends in similar terms. The reference to pheasants in the last line is to the tune "The Pheasant Flies at Dawn" 雉朝飛, which was written for the zither and in which the pheasant is the spirit of a deceased wife who died in a foreign land. Here, Liu and his friends are the pheasants and can't bear sights associated with love and desire. They're all exiles and not likely to see their loved ones again. Liu's own wife died before he left Ch'ang-an, and his mother died shortly after he arrived in Yungchou. (1222)

35. ODE TO RELEASING FRANCOLINS 放鷓鴣詞

Here in the South there's a sweet fat bird
because of its sound we call it a "che-ku"
seeking a mate or food it doesn't stop to think
the trap is sprung and suddenly it's in a net
it breaks its feathers against the bars of its cage
frightened by smoke from the kitchen
adding herbs at the stove to heighten the flavor
the chef waves his hands while assistants look on
the King of Ch'i couldn't bear a trembling cow
Master Chien of Hantan let the pigeons go
in the midst of their joy they thought about such things
what about an exile a thousand miles from home
if I could break my bars and spread my wings
I wouldn't look back even if colleagues called

楚越有鳥甘且腴，嘲嘲自名為鷓鴣。循媒得食不復慮，機械潛發罹置罝。
羽毛摧折觸籠籞，煙火煏赫驚庖廚。鼎前芍藥調五味，膳父攘腕左右視。
齊王不忍觳觫牛，簡子亦放邯鄲鳩。二子得意猶念此，況我萬里為孤囚。
破籠展翅當遠去，同類相呼莫相顧。

....

NOTE: Written in Yungchou in 808. The bird in the poem is a *Francolinus pintadeanus,* or Chinese francolin, which is similar to a chukar or small pheasant. In *Mencius* 孟子 (1A.7), the king of Ch'i is said to have once seen a cow being led to a sacrifice and asked the man to let it go. He said he couldn't bear to see it trembling, knowing it was being led to its death and having committed no offense. There's a similar story in *Liehtzu* 列子 (8.29). Because it was New Year's, the people of Hantan presented Master Chien with some pigeons to eat. When he let them go, the people were confounded and asked why. Chien-tzu said, "Since life begins anew on New Year's Day, it's only fitting to show some kindness." Unmoved, the people told Chien-tzu they had gone to a lot of trouble to catch the birds and asked if letting them go was not tantamount to prohibiting the catching of pigeons, to which Chien-tzu replied, "Indeed, so it is." (1247)

36. Transplanting a Dozen Cassias from Hengyang to My Hermitage in Lingling
自衡陽移桂十餘本植零陵所住精舍

Banished to the southern frontier
past the sacred peak where the Hsiang River winds
I climbed the rush-lined shore at dawn
beneath a cloudless autumn sky
I found some cassias hidden in the weeds
overjoyed I dug them up
from charred ash-covered fields
cleared for firewood long ago
by the roadside they'd gone unnoticed
but the peak is now behind them
their soil was intact when I unpacked them
they were hoping to become home to a phoenix
but the palace on the moon was too far away
and they knew what to do when it rained
people in the South admire them now
who would have known but for me
my innermost thoughts I can't share
but it doesn't help keeping them inside

謫官去南裔，清湘繞靈岳。晨登兼葭岸，霜景霽紛濁。
離披得幽桂，芳本欣盈握。火耕困煙燼，薪採久摧剝。
道旁且不顧，岑嶺況悠邈。傾筐壅故壤，棲息期鸞鷟。
路遠清涼官，一雨悟無學。南人始珍重，微我誰先覺。
芳意不可傳，丹心徒自渥。

....

NOTE: Written in Yungchou in the fall of 808. Liu apparently dug up these plants on his way into exile in the winter of 805. Once he arrived in Yung-chou, he wasn't allowed to travel outside the prefecture, and Hengyang was 150 kilometers to the north. Here they are two years later at his monastic residence and doing quite well. The phoenix appears when a benevolent ruler is on the throne, but it only alights on a paulownia. The cassia is more closely identified with transcendence. There's one on the moon beneath which a rabbit pounds the elixir of immortality. But since the moon is too far away, waiting for the emperor to make use of his branches is the best Liu can hope for. (1231)

VI. Letter of Congratulations to Scholar Wang Ts'an-yuan on the Conflagration 賀進士王參元矢火書

In a letter from Yang Pa, I learned about the fire and that your house had burned. When I first heard, I was alarmed, but then I thought about it and in the end was overjoyed. Hence I've changed my message of condolences to one of congratulations. Given the distance from here and the brevity of the letter, I still don't know the details. But if everything was completely destroyed and there's nothing left, then I congratulate you all the more.

You've worked hard to care for your parents and to make sure their days and nights would be peaceful—your one hope that they would be happy and uneventful ones. Thinking about the devastation of the flames and the trauma to all concerned and that you might even lack the means with which to prepare food, I was alarmed at first. But people say the coming and going of abundance and want or of success and failure can't be stopped, and that those who would do something noteworthy encounter obstacles and alarms at the beginning, and only by suffering the disasters of fire and flood or the abuse of the crowd and the small-minded and by enduring change can one's light shine forth, and that this was true of the ancients. Although the sages wouldn't necessarily agree with the scope or generality of such statements, I thought about this.

You've studied the works of the ancients and write with style and are adept at the lesser studies, but because you're not alone in this regard, you've been unable to rise above the crowd for no other reason than your high status. When people in the capital talk about your family's wealth, officials known for their love of incorruptibility are fearful and don't dare say anything good about you but keep their thoughts to themselves and hide their feelings and avoid expressing themselves because the public is hard to fathom, and people these days are jealous. If someone ever said anything good, people would gossip about bribes.

I first read your writings in the fifteenth year of the Chenyuan period [799], and I've thought about them for nearly seven years without mentioning it. I was focused on myself and turned my back on the public and not just on you. Later, when I served as an attendant censor and was fortunate enough to join the emperor's inner circle, I had opportunities to

speak freely, and I thought about discussing your difficulty. But whenever
I spoke of this with my colleagues, they looked at me and laughed in pri-
vate. I have long been upset that your character has remained unknown
and your reputation overshadowed by the suspicions of the times, and
I've often felt ill at ease speaking about this with Meng Chi-tao. But now
by means of this purifying fire of Heaven, the doubts of the masses have
been utterly extinguished. With your house in ashes and your walls rub-
ble, you clearly have nothing left, and your abilities and talents can now
shine forth untarnished. The truth has been revealed. You've been blessed
by the Fire God. A single night of flames has done more for your reputa-
tion than ten years of friendship with Chi-tao and myself. Now that this
is clear, those who have kept you in their hearts can speak up, and those
who confer assignments won't fear honoring you. Although they might
have preferred to conceal their embarrassment in the past, how can they
continue to do so? From now on I shall expect more of you. This is why
I finally feel so happy.

In the past, when a disaster occurred in one of the states, the other rulers
would send condolences, and when the ruler of Hsu failed to do so, the gen-
tlemen of the land reviled him. What I've expressed here is similar, although
it's also different from this ancient example; hence I've changed my condo-
lences to congratulations. If the happiness Master Yen and Master Tseng
enjoyed in caring for their parents was great, why should yours be any less?

得楊八書，知足下遇火災，家無餘儲。僕始聞而駭，中而疑，終乃大喜，蓋將
弔而更以賀也。道遠言略，猶未能究知其狀。若果蕩焉泯焉而悉無有，乃吾所
以尤賀者也。

足下勤奉養，寧朝夕，唯恬安無事是望。乃今有焚煬赫烈之虞，以震駭左
右，而脂膏滫瀡之具，或以不給，吾是以始而駭也。凡人之言皆曰盈虛倚伏，
去來之不可常。或將大有為也，乃始厄困震悸，於是有水火之孽，有群小之
慍，勞苦變動，而後能光明，古之人皆然。斯道遼闊誕漫，雖聖人不能以是必
信，是故中而疑也。

以足下讀古人書，為文章，善小學，其為多能若是，而進不能出群士之
上，以取顯貴者，無他故焉。京城人多言足下家有積貨，士之好廉名者，皆畏
忌，不敢道足下之善，獨自得之，心蓄之，銜忍而不出諸口，以公道之難明，
而世之多嫌也。一出口，則嗤嗤者以為得重賂。

僕自貞元十五年見足下之文章，蓄之者蓋六七年未嘗言。是僕私一身而負
公道久矣，非特負足下也。及為御史尚書郎，自以幸為天子近臣，得奮其舌，

思以發明足下之鬱塞。然時稱道於行列，猶有顧視而竊笑者。僕良恨修己之不亮，素譽之不立，而為世嫌之所加，常與孟幾道言而痛之。乃今幸為天火之所滌蕩，凡眾之疑慮，舉為灰埃。黔其廬，赭其垣，以示其無有，而足下之才能乃可顯白而不污。其實出矣。是祝融回祿之相吾子也。則僕與幾道十年之相知，不若茲火一夕之為足下譽也。宥而彰之，使夫蓄於心者，咸得開其喙，發策決科者，授子而不慄。雖欲如向之蓄縮受侮，其可得乎。於茲吾有望乎爾。是以終乃大喜也。

　　古者列國有災，同位者皆相吊，許不弔災，君子惡之。今吾之所陳若是，有以異乎古，故將弔而更以賀也。顏曾之養，其為樂也大矣，又何闕焉。

....

NOTE: Written in Yungchou in 808. Wang Ts'an-yuan was a younger brother of Wang Mao-yuan 王茂元 (d. 843). Their father was Wang Ch'i-yao 王棲曜 (d. 803) who served in a number of high posts under Emperor Te-tsung (d. 805). Yang Pa (or Ching-chih 敬之) was Liu's brother-in-law and was still living in the capital, as he had just passed the imperial exam the previous year and was waiting for an appointment. Meng Chi-tao (d. 824), aka Meng Chien 孟簡, was one of Liu's closest friends during his time at court. At the time Liu wrote this letter, Meng was serving as the director of the Bureau of Honors. Yen Hui 顏回 was Confucius's favorite disciple, and Tseng Ts'an 曾參 was the Sage's successor. Both were known for their devotion to their parents. (862)

37. AT NIGHT IN EARLY AUTUMN, FOR WU WU-LING
初秋夜坐贈吳武陵

Gusts of mist blow through the bamboo
magpies flutter in the bushes
my friend is on the Hsiang's far shore
but the autumn wind lasts all night
the fog is too thick to see through
and the cresting waves never end
I can't say the one I miss is far
but I'm not with him tonight
a lover of uncommon music
his paulownia plank strung with red silk
notes rising from the Western Vault
then surging across the sky
spontaneous not contrived
the work of Heaven not effort
simplicity hidden in the subtlest of sounds
something a deaf fool wouldn't understand

稍稍雨侵竹，翻翻鵲驚叢。美人隔湘浦，一夕生秋風。
積霧杳難極，滄波浩無窮。相思豈云遠，即席莫與同。
若人抱奇音，朱弦綰枯桐。清商激西顥，泛灩凌長空。
自得本無作，天成諒非功。希聲閟大樸，聾俗何由聰。

....

NOTE: Written in Yungchou in the fall of 808. Wu Wu-ling (d. 834) was banished to Yungchou earlier that year and became one of Liu's most frequent companions. Wu settled on the west shore of the Hsiao (here referred to as the Hsiang), across from Liu's residence at Lunghsing Temple. Wu returned to the capital in 812 and later asked Chancellor P'ei Tu 裴度 to arrange a pardon for Liu, but to no avail. Both Liu and Wu were adept at playing the zither, or ku-ch'in 古琴. For such instruments, paulownia wood was prized for its lightness as well as its sound. Until modern times, zithers were strung with silk thread. The softer sound was intended for friends, not neighbors. The forces of autumn are said to rise from the Western Vault of Heaven. (1134)

38. Red Banana 紅蕉

Its bloom lasts until year-end
its glossy leaves harbor a red glow
a color from the height of summer
a beauty that overcomes the cold
people love things from far away
but such things cause a traveler pain
as I look through the woods at dusk
not a single flower remains

晚英值窮節，綠潤含朱光。以茲正陽色，窈窕凌清霜。
遠物世所重，旅人心獨傷。回暉眺林際，戚戚無遺芳。

....

NOTE: Written in Yungchou in the winter of 808. The red banana, or *Musa coccinea,* is a member of the plantain family. It produces a cluster of red bracts, but nothing resembling a banana. According to the twelfth-century poet Fan Ch'eng-ta 范成大, its fragrance lasts from midsummer until the beginning of spring. (1234)

39. Lingling Spring View 零陵春望

Spring grass has turned the countryside green
orioles are singing in the distant woods
dawn lights the Hsiaohsiang's sandbars
clouds obscure Koulou Peak
waiting for immortals is hopeless
a worldly career is beyond my reach
reflecting on what I love is futile
beneath a thousand miles of Tsangwu shade

平野春草綠，曉鶯啼遠林。日晴瀟湘渚，雲斷岣嶁岑。
仙駕不可望，世途非所任。凝情空景慕，萬里蒼梧陰。

....

NOTE: Written in Yungchou most likely in the spring of 809. Lingling was an
old name for Yungchou and is the name by which the old town is still known.
The town was on the east shore of the Hsiao River, which was met by the
Hsiang just north of town, at which point their combined waters are some-
times referred to as the Hsiaohsiang. Koulou is the name of the main peak
of the sacred mountain of Hengshan. This was where Yu the Great 大禹 (ca.
2200 BC) received instructions from the immortals. A hundred and fifty
kilometers northeast of Lingling as the crow flies, it would have been a very
distant view, assuming the clouds permitted. Mount Tsangwu was a hundred
kilometers to the south and was where Emperor Shun (ca. 2250 BC) was bur-
ied. In Liu's day, Emperor Shun and Yu the Great were the heroes of those
hoping to reform the government. Their examples are what Liu reflects on in
the penultimate line. (1218)

40. REBURYING THE BONES OF WORKMAN CHANG CHIN 掩役夫張進骸

Birth and death go on forever
breath fills this body then it's gone
meanwhile there's joy and anger
suddenly it's goodbye again
why look down on a workman
his betters weren't that much better
one day there was no sign of life
no beauty or ugliness only decay
he spent his life cleaning stables
he didn't complain cutting hay
when he died they gave him a cheap coffin
then buried him at the foot of East Mountain
but there's no stopping erosion
the slope above the roadway collapsed
his bones were suddenly exposed
too scattered to put back together
luckily a passerby told me
when I saw for myself I cried
tigers and cats are invoked at a funeral
horses and dogs are covered with a shroud
all I did was stand there and sigh
how could I not do more
I got a shovel a basket and a marker
I dug a ditch to protect the site
at least it brought me some peace
and I didn't think he would mind
reburying bones occurs in the spring
and this was that time of year
I wasn't here to do anything else
why not look after his things

生死悠悠爾，一氣聚散之。偶來紛喜怒，奄忽已復辭。
為役孰賤辱，為貴非神奇。一朝纊息定，枯朽無妍媸。
生平勤皂櫪，到秣不告疲。既死給槥櫝，葬之東山基。
奈何值崩湍，蕩析臨路垂。髐然暴百骸，散亂不復支。
從者幸告余，睠之涓然悲。貓虎獲迎祭，犬馬有蓋帷。
佇立唅爾魂，豈復識此為。畚鍤載埋瘞，溝瀆護其危。
我心得所安，不謂爾有知。掩骼著春令，茲焉適其時。
及物非吾輩，聊且顧爾私。

....

NOTE: Written in Yungchou in the late spring of 809. People visit ancestral graves to pay their respects at the beginning of the third lunar month, 108 days after the winter solstice. Tigers and cats were invoked at funerals to drive off vermin. When dogs or horses died, their bodies were wrapped in a shroud. All Mister Chang got was a coffin that fell apart when the slope where he was buried subsided. Liu was still living at Lunghsing Temple. During the entire time he was in Yungchou, he had no official duties. He simply followed his interests, as here. (1261)

41. FEELING DECREPIT 覺衰

I knew old age would find me
I never guessed I would watch it arrive
I shouldn't be decrepit so young
but I'm beginning to see the signs
like gaps in my teeth and thinning hair
and not enough stamina to run
but what good is complaining
at least my mind hasn't been affected
and where are P'eng-tsu and Lao-tzu
Confucius or the Duke of Chou
the ones we call centenarians or sages
none of them is alive today
all I want is good wine
and a few friends to share it with
spring is nearly over
the fruit trees have already leafed out
the sun is shining and the sky is pure blue
hearing a migrating swan in the distance
I walked out my door and yelled to my friends
"Grab your canes we're off to the woods
let's have some fun and try singing
those ancient lines from the Odes of Shang"

久知老會至，不謂便見侵。今年宜未衰，稍已來相尋。
齒疏髮就種，奔走力不任。咄此可奈何，未必傷我心。
彭聃安在哉，周孔亦已沉。古稱壽聖人，曾不留至今。
但願得美酒，朋友常共斟。是時春向暮，桃李生繁陰。
日照天正綠，杳杳歸鴻吟。出門呼所親，扶杖發西林。
高歌足自快，商頌有遺音。

....

NOTE: Written in Yungchou in the late spring of 809, most likely not long after the previous poem, when Liu would have been a mere thirty-seven. P'eng-tsu 彭祖 was said to have lived 800 years, or nearly all of the third millennium BC, and Lao-tzu was a Taoist sage of the first millennium BC. The Duke of Chou 周公 and Confucius also lived in the first millennium BC and were the patriarchs of what later became known as Confucianism. Liu was still living at Lunghsing Temple. Hence, the friends he yells to were most likely the coterie of fellow exiles who were also availing themselves of its lodgings. The "Sacrificial Odes of Shang" were included in a section in the Book of Poetry edited by Confucius and date back to the second millennium BC, if not earlier. According to Chuang-tzu (*Chuangtzu* 28), these particular odes were the favorite poems of Tseng-tzu 曾子, Confucius's successor, who liked to chant them to ameliorate his hardships. They were usually chanted with drums and gongs and with little concern for their meaning. (1198)

42. Plum Rains 梅雨

Plums turn ripe when the monsoon arrives
when the sky disappears in late spring
gibbons add to my depression at night
roosters shatter my dreams at dawn
ocean fog covers the South Pole
river clouds obscure the North Ford
the reason my clothes aren't white anymore
isn't capital dust

梅實迎時雨，蒼茫值晚春。愁深楚猿夜，夢斷越雞晨。
海霧連南極，江雲暗北津。素衣今盡化，非為帝京塵。

....

NOTE: Written in Yungchou in the early summer of 809. Plums ripen in
the fifth lunar month, which is also the rainy season in the Yangtze water-
shed. Gibbons and their howls kept exiled poets awake in Central and South
China until as recently as the Ming dynasty (1368–1644). They've since been
reduced to a few isolated nature reserves along China's southern border. The
South Pole refers to Canopus, the southern polar star, which was not visible
in North China, and the North Ford refers to Polaris, the northern polar
star. The capital of Ch'ang-an was known for its dust, while South China was
known for its mud, especially during the monsoon season. (1237)

VII. Preface to the Poems Titled "Drinking at Night at Fahua Temple's West Pavilion"

法華寺西亭夜飲賦詩序

After I was exiled to Yungchou, because the western edge of Fahua Monastery looked out on a pond and hillside as well as a great river and a chain of mountains that were accessible despite their height and visible despite their distance, I cut down some of the trees and built a pavilion that faced the wind and rain so I could view the beginning of creation and imagine the birth of the firmament. The following year, Yuan K'e-chi arrived after being demoted from his post in the Censorate. Not long after that other literary friends began showing up. Assembled here tonight at this pavilion are eight of us. And now that we're drunk, K'e-chi wants to record this meeting for posterity and has commanded us all to write poems and for me to write a preface.

In the past, when Chao Meng visited the state of Cheng, he asked seven scholars to record the sights in the kingdom, and is K'e-chi not an admirer of Chao? Pu Tzu-hsia then wrote a preface for their poems, which enabled later generations to appreciate the elegant style of that time, and am I not an admirer of Pu? If what we have written should actually be transmitted to later ages, then in some small manner we will have approached those ancients.

余既謫永州，以法華浮圖之西臨陂池丘陵，大江連山，其高可以上，其遠可以望，遂伐木為亭，以臨風雨，觀物初，而游乎顥氣之始。間歲，元克己由柱下亦謫焉而來。無幾何，以文從余者多萃焉。是夜，會茲亭者凡八人。既醉，克己欲志是會以貽于後，咸命為詩，而授余序。

昔趙孟至於鄭，賦七子以觀鄭志，克己其慕趙者歟。卜子夏為詩序，使後世知風雅之道，余其慕卜者歟。誠使斯文也而傳于世，庶乎其近於古矣。

....

Note: The poems Chao Meng and his friends wrote around 500 BC were recorded in the anthology compiled by Confucius known as the Book of Poetry, for which his disciple Pu Tzu-hsia wrote a preface. The only poem written on this occasion that survived is the one Liu wrote, poem 43. (645)

43. DRINKING AT NIGHT AT FAHUA TEMPLE'S WEST PAVILION 法華寺西亭夜飲

Sunset at the pavilion in Jetavana Garden
all of us drinking meditation wine
beyond the steps a fog-shrouded pond
moonlit flowers in the windows
let's not disparage getting drunk tonight
so far no one here has white hair

祇樹夕陽亭，共傾三昧酒。霧暗水連堦，月明花覆牖。
莫厭罇前醉，相看未白首。

....

NOTE: Written in Yungchou in 809. Jetavana Garden was located on the outskirts of the ancient Indian city of Sravasti and was the scene of numerous expositions by the Buddha, including the *Lotus Sutra,* after which this temple (Fahua: Dharma Flower) is named. Liu built this pavilion the previous year (see poem 12). It was located at the western edge of the temple grounds and overlooked the rooftops of Yungchou, the 300-meter-wide waters of the Hsiao, and the mountains beyond. Buddhist monasteries often used euphemisms as expedient means to permit what were felt to be inconsequential violations of the rules. Meals after midday, for example, are normally forbidden for monks and nuns but allowed as "medicine." Here, "meditation wine" would seem to fall under this category for visiting laymen. Liu was thirty-seven when he wrote this. Not long afterward, he began complaining about the changing color of his hair. (1222)

44. READING BOOKS 讀書

Living in obscurity I've given up current affairs
I bow my head in silence and reflect on the sage kings
the highs and lows of the ancient past
the ups and downs of countless paths
I laugh to myself when I'm pleased
when I'm sad I simply sigh
I take my books from their cases
I go through from front to back
despite the affliction of tropical diseases
I feel different than in the past
while reading I suddenly understand
when I'm done my mind is a blank
who can I talk with at night
if not these texts on bamboo and silk
I lie down when I get tired
after a good sleep I feel refreshed
I yawn and stretch my limbs
I read out loud to my heart's content
I enjoy doing what suits me
not to please learned men
I shut up when I've said what I want
free of restraints I relax
the clever consider me stupid
the wise think I'm a fool
but reading has managed to make me happy
what good is working till you drop
cherish this body of yours
don't use it to chase after fame

幽沉謝世事，俛默窺唐虞。上下觀古今，起伏千萬途。
遇欣或自笑，感戚亦以吁。縹帙各舒散，前後互相逾。
瘴痾擾靈府，日與往昔殊。臨文乍了了，徹券兀若無。
竟夕誰與言，但與竹素俱。倦極更倒臥，熟寐乃一蘇。
欠伸展肢體，吟咏心自愉。得意適其適，非願為世儒。

道盡即閉口，蕭散損囚拘。巧者為我拙，智者為我愚。
書史足自悅，安用勤與劬。貴爾六尺軀，勿為名所驅。

....

NOTE: Written in Yungchou in 809. Liu wrote to friends that during this and the previous year he read several hundred volumes. Finally, Liu sees the silver lining in his rustication. The use of hemp and other plant fibers to make paper began around two thousand years ago during the Han dynasty. During the T'ang, the most common fibers used in paper production were from bamboo, which were in turn replaced by mulberry bark in the Sung (960–1279). Works that were more highly prized were copied onto silk. The sage kings of the third millennium BC were Liu's heroes: Fu Hsi, Yao, Shun, and Yu the Great. It was during his years in Yungchou that Liu produced the works that made him one of the two greatest essayists of the T'ang, his contemporary and friend Han Yu being the other. (1254)

45. ODE TO THREE GOOD MEN 詠三良

Wearing court attire they met the Bright Lord
his every look radiated light
they exerted themselves with one mind
establishing the hegemony of Ch'in
they served with loyalty and devotion
their mutual affection shone like snow
in life they were truly one
how could they be apart in death
they joined him in his grave in their prime
their aspirations ended up in their coffins
the problem with dying with one's lord
especially when it included such men
Ch'in's moral rule was thereby eclipsed
the might of Chin and Ch'u grew stronger
illness surely muddles the mind
this was Wei's son's view
but "obeying a wrong they wronged their own fathers"
I wish I could talk to that madman

束帶值明后，顧盼流輝光。一心在陳力，鼎列夸四方。
款款効忠信，恩義皎如霜。生時亮同體，死沒寧分張。
壯軀閉幽隨，猛志填黃腸。殉死禮所非，況乃用其良。
霸基弊不振，晉楚更張皇。疾病命固亂，魏氏言有章。
從邪陷厥父，吾欲討彼狂。

....

NOTE: Written in Yungchou in 809, most likely after reading poems with the
same title and on the same theme by Tsao Chih 曹植 and T'ao Yuan-ming. The
Three Good Men refer to three brothers: Yen-hsi 奄息, Chung-hsing 仲行, and
Chen-hu 鍼虎. All three served at the court of Duke Mu 穆公, who ruled the
state of Ch'in and who was called the Bright Lord. When the duke died, they
joined him in death. There were a number a states competing for hegemony at
this time, and Duke Mu's decision to ask his advisers to accompany him into
the grave appalled many and led to the temporary elevation in people's minds

of the rulers of the two competing states of Chin and Ch'u. Liu also cites Duke Hsuan 宣公 of the state of Wei. When he became ill, he asked his son to marry his favorite concubine after he died. But as his illness progressed, the duke changed his mind and told his son to bury the woman with him. Wei's son ignored his father, claiming his father's illness had muddled his mind, and he proceded to marry the woman as directed earlier. While Liu doesn't object to Duke Hsuan's son's reasoning, he does in the case of Duke Mu's son, Duke K'ang 康公, who said the decision of the three officials to accompany his father in death was an offense against their own fathers. Liu sees Duke K'ang's view as an offense against his own father, but he also sees something else. He sees his mentor, Wang Shu-wen, the leader of the reform faction of which he was a member, in the same light as the Three Good Men—his suicide (forced) being the proper thing to do. He also sees Emperor Hsien-tsung as not following the wishes of his father, Emperor Shun-tsung, the reform faction's greatest supporter, who was forced by his son to abdicate following a stroke. Of course, for Liu to state this clearly would have been an example of lèse-majesté and would have led to his own suicide, if not execution. (1258)

46. Ode for Ching K'e 詠荊軻

Yen and Ch'in couldn't both exist
this worried the crown prince of Yen
a reward of gold provided a plan

he would send Ching K'e with a dagger
all year long Yen gave what Ch'in asked
the prospects were war or slaughter
meanwhile a plot arose out of anger
Ching K'e left full of rage
beside the Yi River facing the North Wind
he drained his cup and spurred his horse on
he brought the head of a traitor
then he unrolled a map of the lands
there was suddenly a flash of light
he thrust his dagger but missed
as events unfolded what was the use
when the moment came he hesitated
like a rainbow appearing on a sunny day
it turned out it was Ching K'e who died
the king grabbed his sword and vented his wrath
his shouts accompanied by wind and thunder
the king of Yen killed his own son
he fled but there was no place to hide
the capital was razed and the royal family slaughtered
the palace was burned to the ground
Yen worried at first about disaster
in the end disaster arrived
the king of Ch'in was utterly ruthless
unlike Duke Huan of Ch'i
but Ts'ao Mo isn't a good example
just being brave is foolish
such tales always include the absurd
the physician was the Historian's choice

燕秦不兩立，太子已為虞。千金奉短計，匕首荊卿趨。
窮年徇所欲，兵勢且見屠。微言激幽憤，怒目辭燕都。
朔風動易水，揮爵前長驅。函首致宿怨，獻田開版圖。
炯然耀電光，掌握罔正夫。造端何其銳，臨事竟趑趄。
長虹吐白日，蒼卒反受誅。按劍赫憑怒，風雷助號呼。
慈父斷子首，狂走無容軀。夷城芟七族，臺觀皆焚污。
始期憂患弭，卒動災禍樞。秦皇本詐力，事與桓公殊。
奈何效曹子，實謂勇且愚。世傳故多謬，太史徵無且。

....

NOTE: Written in Yungchou in 809. Again, Liu was inspired by a poem with the same title on the same theme by T'ao Yuan-ming, as well as accounts of these events in the histories he was reading. Ching K'e was an assassin in the employ of the crown prince of Yen. The plot conceived by the prince was for the assassin to present the head of a man who had betrayed the state of Ch'in along with a map of territory to be ceded but to hide a dagger in the scroll. Such was the king of Ch'in's paranoia, no one at the Ch'in court was allowed to carry a weapon except him. As the map was unrolled, Ching K'e grabbed the dagger and thrust it forward. But it was too short to do the job, and the king retreated behind a pillar. As Ching K'e tried to pursue the king, Wu-chu, the royal physician, thwarted the assassination by throwing bags of medicine at Ching K'e, which gave the king time to recover and unsheathe his own sword, with which he then wounded the assassin. Armed guards finally arrived and finished the job. At the end of the poem, Liu cites Duke Huan 桓公 of Ch'i as an example of honesty and leniency, in contrast to the king of Ch'in, who would go on to become China's infamous First Emperor. Ts'ao Mo 曹沫 was a general in the state of Lu 魯. At a treaty ceremony where lands Ts'ao Mo was responsible for losing were to become officially part of Ch'i territory, Ts'ao grabbed Duke Huan and held a knife to his throat and threatened to kill him if he didn't renounce his claim and give back the lands. Huan agreed, and the lands were returned, and Ts'ao has been praised ever since. No one seems to have blamed him for losing the territory in the first place. This and much more can be found in the *Records of the Historian* 史記, compiled around 200 BC by Ssu-ma Ch'ien, in which China's early history is recounted in the light of Confucian morality. Ching K'e is thus presented as an example of an unsuccessful assassin, and Ts'ao Mo as an example of a "successful" one. Between the lines here, Liu sees the T'ang court pursuing policies similar to those of the ruthless king of Ch'in, whose would-be assassin becomes an ill-fated hero, and whose physician is ridiculed for having protected such a man. (1259)

47. With Vice Censor-in-Chief Ts'ui Passing District Defender Lu's Country Home

從崔中丞過盧少府郊居

He lives without neighbors near the banks of the Hsiang
the world can't ensnare a man who esteems himself
in his uncluttered yard he plants the statesman
inside his empty house he pours the scholar
his spring ripples over rocks and beneath willows
his path wanders through bamboo and green vines
a Taoist adept of the beast and bird forms
wherever he goes gulls follow him around

寓居湘岸四無鄰，世網難嬰每自珍。a蒔藥閑庭延國老，開罇虛室值賢人。
泉迴淺石依高柳，逕轉垂藤間綠筠。聞道偏為五禽戲，出門鷗鳥更相親。

....

Note: Written in Yungchou in 809. Ts'ui Min was Liu's maternal uncle. He was appointed magistrate of Yungchou in 808 and died there in the fall of 810. Liu uses the title Ts'ui held previous to his appointment. While he was living in Yungchou, Ts'ui chose to live on the west shore of the Hsiao, where Liu himself moved not long after he wrote this poem. As elsewhere, Liu refers to the river by the name it aquired just north of town, where it was joined by the Hsiang. As for Lu Tsun, he was Liu's cousin and Ts'ui's nephew. After accompaning Liu to Yungchou in 805, he remained there. His residence was up a side stream also on the west shore of the Hsiao across from the city's Taiping Gate 太平門. Among herbs, licorice was known as "the statesman." Cloudy, unfiltered rice wine was known as "the scholar," and clear, filtered rice wine was called "the sage." The five animal-like movements originally devised in the Han dynasty by the Taoist physician Hua T'uo 花佗 mimicked those of tigers, deer, bears, monkeys, and birds. The seagull reference is from the Taoist text known as *Liehtzu* (2.13), in which a fisherman is followed during his daily walk on the beach by seagulls until someone asks him to try catching one. (1219)

48. AT HSIANGKOU INN, WHERE THE HSIAO AND HSIANG MEET 湘口館瀟湘二水所會

Racing forth from the slopes of Chiuyi
winding through the glens of Linyuan
becoming one with the boundless
their thunder ends in transparent depths
above the inn I gazed into space
from the railing I looked down on ravines
the weather this morning finally cleared
even the wispiest clouds were gone
the sun was shining in an autumn sky
the water was a flawless jade-green
in the distance a fisherman was singing
a wintering crane was calling
but I couldn't enjoy such a transcendent scene

I couldn't stop thinking of my separation
I was hoping I could relax this high up
but I thought about the distance even more
the current was flowing strong and wide
and boats weren't taking their time

九疑濬傾奔，臨源委縈迴。會合屬空曠，泓澄停風雷。
高館軒霞表，危樓臨山隈。茲辰始澂霽，纖雲盡褰開。
天秋日正中，水碧無塵埃。杳杳漁父吟，叫叫羇鴻哀。
境勝豈不豫，慮分固難裁。升高欲自舒，彌使遠念來。
歸流駛且廣，汎舟絕沿迴。

....

NOTE: Written in Yungchou in the fall of 809 during a visit to a government
inn north of town that overlooked the place where the Hsiao was joined by
the Hsiang. For Liu this was where the way home began. The source of the
Hsiao is on Chiuyi Mountain, and the Hsiang begins on Mount Linyuan.
(1190)

49. Crossing a Small Ridge on Shihchiao on the Way to Changwu Village 遊石角過小嶺至長烏村

To be honored was never my goal
the Way can't survive an expedient life
I disdained life at court long ago
I ridiculed the path to immortality too
a banished official on the banks of the Hsiang
an irresolute mind flaps from my banner
I was startled at first by the duplicity of the times
I'm just trying now to escape Heaven's wrath
I worry about the vanishing years
lazy and withdrawn I seldom receive guests
I made this excursion thinking I'd enjoy it
also to give vent to my feelings
I chose Shihchiao's less-traveled path
Changwu was a good long hike
stone steps wound through dense woods
icy streams reflected a cloudless sky
the vistas were grand and people few
I heard a crane calling in a field
through wind-bent bamboo I saw the distant river
frost-covered paddies encroaching below the hill
having little to do with worldly affairs
I view this life of mine lightly
farmers are more apt to be happy
the glory of court favorites is vain
great trees were common in ancient times
I just hope I can stay true
and get this body back to the fields
to farm that east hill is my goal

志適不期貴，道存豈偷生。久忘上封事，復笑昇天行。
竄逐宦湘浦，搖心劇懸旌。始驚陷世議，終欲逃天刑。
歲月殺憂慄，慵疏寡將迎。追遊疑所愛，且復舒吾情。
石角恣幽步，長烏遂遐征。磴迴茂樹斷，景晏寒川明。

曠望少行人，時聞田鶴鳴。風篁冒水遠，霜稻侵山平。
稍與人事間，益知身世輕。為農信可樂，居寵真虛榮。
喬木餘故國，願言果丹誠。四支反田畝，釋志東皋耕。

....

NOTE: Written in Yungchou in the fall of 809. Shihchiao was a small hill 2 kilometers northeast of Lunghsing Temple and just beyond the town's city wall. Except for a single rocky outcrop, it has lately been bulldozed into submission by a high-end housing development. Changwu Village was located at the northeast foot of the hill and has since been replaced by Mayuan Village 麻園村. The "east hill" refers to land farmed by the poet-recluse T'ao Yuanming near his hermitage at the southeast foot of Lushan. (1193)

50. PLANTING THISTLES 種朮

In my forced leisure I've begun eating herbs
in Tungshan's ravines I pick thistles
in the mountain's steep and darker places
I've searched until I'm exhausted
I dig up their miraculous roots with care
protecting their natural forms
I take them from rock-lined streams
to join the sedge in my garden
where the soil is rich and especially moist
where dew drips down from the pines
now a whole field faces the sun
a winding confusion of interlocking branches
I walk past their flowers in the morning
their scent is still strong at night
I wish they could cure homesickness
but who knows all that they do
when I cook bamboo shoots I add their sweet leaves
I no longer worry about consumption or plague
some people compose poems about growing irises
others hum songs about picking ferns
aware of my stupidity I am who I am
I regret the reforms dragged others down too
Tan Pao focused on correcting himself
what good did a big door do

守閑事服餌，採朮東山阿。東山幽且阻，疲苶煩經過。
戒徒斸靈根，對植閟天和。違爾澗底石，徹我庭中莎。
土膏滋玄液，松露墜繁柯。南東自成畝，繚繞紛相羅。
晨步佳色媚，夜眠幽氣多。離憂苟可怡，孰能知其他。
爨竹茹芳蕈，寧慮瘵與痾。留連樹蕙辭，婉娩採薇歌。
悟拙甘自足，激清愧同波。單豹且理內，高門復如何。

....

NOTE: Written in Yungchou in the fall of 809. In Chinese medicine, this-tles (*Atractylodes macrocephala*) are used for strengthening the body and improving digestion. The most common variety in China has white flow-ers. Ch'u Yuan wrote poems about growing irises during his exile. The two recluses Po Yi and Shu-ch'i 叔齊 sang songs about picking ferns. Near the end of this poem, Liu finds himself content with the simplicity of his life in exile but feels remorse that he dragged his friends into the reform movement that got them all banished. The references in the last two lines are from *Chuangtzu* 19.5: Tan Pao 單豹 focused on inner cultivation and lived to be seventy, while Chang Yi 張毅 built an unusually big door to make people think he was a man to be reckoned with, but he was so successful he died of overwork before he was forty—Liu was thirty-seven when he wrote this. In reconsidering his career as an official, Liu sees Tan Pao as a salutary model and Chang Yi as a cautionary one. (1226)

51. Planting a Lingshou Tree 植靈壽木

Seeing my white hair in an icy stream
I was relieved to be in the countryside
walking along I asked an old man
who repeated this delightful name
since becoming lame and decrepit
and quitting work in my prime
not waiting for the gift of a cane
I decided to transplant one of these
while my garden flowers were showing off
it opened its buds outside my room
its drooping stem soon straightened
it grew stronger and multiplied
when I use one of these my feet don't feel tired
my steps have begun to feel lighter
and it doesn't need to be shortened
it's the perfect thing for a hike

白華鑒寒水，怡我適野情。前趨問長老，重復欣嘉名。
蹇連易衰朽，方剛謝經營。敢期齒杖賜，聊且移孤莖。
叢萼中競秀，分房外舒英。柔條乍反植，勁節常對生。
循玩足忘疲，稍覺步武輕。安能事翦伐，持用資徒行。

....

NOTE: Written in Yungchou in the winter of 809 while Liu was living at Lunghsing Temple. The lingshou (similar to *Viburnum x rhytidophylloides*, "willowwood") produces multiple, jointed, bamboo-like stems about 8 feet long and 3 to 4 inches around. One was once given by an empress to her senior adviser. Since Liu was out of office, he saw no sense in waiting for such a present. Lingshou's "delightful name" in Chinese means "plant of long life." (1230)

52. PLANTING *EPIMEDIUM* 種仙靈毗

Living in poverty I lack nutrition
and this noxious air isn't kind
at the height of winter nothing freezes
at sunset the air is still warm
walking outside with my staff
I limp before reaching the gate
it was there that I met a local official
who came to comfort my troubled spirit
he happened to mention an efficacious plant
it grew right across the river
if I ate it for only a week
my feeble feet would soon dance
I clapped with delight and implored him
to dig up some roots on my behalf
the plants soon covered my yard
their leaves and flowers were everywhere
I picked them in the morning then dried them
I pounded them in a mortar at night
they harmonized the workings of my organs
they attacked the source of my illness
as a plaster they drove away dampness
as a salve they got rid of heat
if I need an example of their special effects
perhaps they're a bit like an iris
I heard there are adepts with powers
who can make one breath last all night
who are able to inhale so deeply
their breath can reach the soles of their feet
this isn't for someone as lazy as me
not when I can take a pill
suffering atrophy I didn't forget how to stand
and I'm not blaming poverty again
this divine plant has restored my legs
I can run around now like a child

窮陋闕自養，癘氣劇嚚煩。隆冬乏霜霰，日夕南風溫。
杖藜下庭際，曳踵不及門。門有野田吏，慰我飄零魂。
及言有靈藥，近在湘西原。服之不盈旬，蹩躠皆騰騫。
笑抃前即吏，為我擢其根。薛薛遂充庭，英翹忽已繁。
晨起自採曝，杵臼通夜喧。靈和理內藏，攻疾貴自源。
甕覆逃積霧，伸舒委餘暄。奇功苟可徵，寧復資蘭蓀。
我聞畸人術，一氣中夜存。能令深深息，呼吸還歸跟。
疏放固難效，且以藥餌論。瘁者不忘起，窮者寧復言。
神哉輔吾足，幸及兒女奔。

....

NOTE: Written in Yungchou in the winter of 809. The leaves of *Epimedium* (horny goat weed) are described as having both energizing and calming effects and are used to treat fatigue and general malaise. Liu suffered from flaccidity and numbness in his legs. (1224)

53. The Janhsi River 冉溪

I used my strength for noble ends when I was young
I worked for the country not for myself
a misstep in a storm and I was sent a thousand miles
my resolution broken a prisoner without a prison
a prisoner my final years with nothing to do
I'm moving to the Janhsi on the west shore of the Hsiang
I'm going to copy Fan Chung the Duke of Shouchang
I'll plant a grove of lacquer trees and wait to be of use

少時陳力希公侯，許國不復為身謀。風波一跌逝萬里，壯心瓦解空縲囚。
縲囚終老無餘事，願卜湘西冉溪地。却學壽張樊敬侯，種漆南園待成器。

....

NOTE: Written in Yungchou in late 809. It was normal for someone exiled
to have their rustication reconsidered after two years and again after five.
Coming up on five years, it was clear to Liu that he would not be returning to

Ch'ang-an, and he began looking for a more permanent place to live. Lung-hsing Temple caught fire four times while he was living there. The place he decided on was the Janhsi, or Dye River, which he renamed the Yuhsi, or Stupid River, to remind him of why he was there. The "misstep" Liu is referring to was the failed reform of 805, of which he was one of the leaders—hence his exile. Fan Chung 樊重 of the Later Han dynasty wanted to create something useful and planted lacquer trees in his garden. Everyone ridiculed him, but when his trees started producing lacquer, people sang his praises. He was later enfeoffed as the Duke of Shouchang and given the posthumous name Ching 敬. (1221)

VIII. Preface to the Yuhsi River Poems 愚溪詩序

North of the waters of the Kuan there's a river that flows east into the Hsiao. Some say the Jan family once lived there, so it was called the Jan-hsi River. Others say it was used for dyeing and that's why it was called the Jan[dye]hsi. Because I committed an offense out of stupidity, I was banished to the Hsiao and fell in love with this tributary and followed it upstream two or three *li* and built a house where it was exceptionally beautiful. Because there was once a place called Mister Stupid's Valley, now that I've made my home on this river, since no one has settled the matter of its name, and locals are still debating it, there was nothing preventing me from changing it, and so I've changed it to Stupid River [Yuhsi].

Along Stupid River, I bought a small hill, which became Stupid Hill. From Stupid Hill, walking northeast sixty paces, I found a spring and purchased it for my home site, and it became Stupid Spring. Stupid Spring consists of six rivulets, all of which come out of a level place at the foot of the mountain. Once they merge, the water flows south, forming Stupid Gully. By piling up dirt and rocks, I blocked the water from escaping and formed Stupid Pond. East of Stupid Pond, I built Stupid Hall, and to the south, I built Stupid Pavilion. In the middle of the pond, I made Stupid Island, where I arranged some exceptionally beautiful trees and rocks to create a wonderful landscape. But because of me all of this has been demeaned as stupid.

Water, of course, is what the wise delight in. So how is it that this river alone has been demeaned as stupid? Because the water level is too low, it can't be used for irrigation. And because the current is too strong and full of boulders, large boats can't go upstream. And because it's too remote, too shallow, and too narrow, dragons can't live there to produce clouds or rain. Of no benefit to the world, it's exactly like me, and so it's only appropriate that I disparage it as being stupid. Ning Wu-tzu lived in a country bereft of the Tao, so he acted stupid. But this was a case of someone wise acting stupid. Master Yen didn't raise objections all day long, as if he were stupid, but this was a case of someone perceptive seeming stupid but not really being stupid. I'm fortunate to live in a time when the Tao prevails, and yet I have offended reason and made a mess of things to the point where no one can compare to me in stupidity. This being so, no one in the realm can argue with me about conferring this name on this river.

While this river is of no benefit to the world, it is, however, good at reflecting countless things. Its purity and transparency and the sound of its music can make a stupid person laugh in delight and sigh in rapture and become so happy he can't leave. Although I don't get along with most people, I manage to comfort myself through writing whereby I purify all of creation and encompass everything without exception. By singing about Stupid River with my stupid expressions and being too ignorant to offend it, I have thereby become completely one with it, have transcended the beginning of time, and have merged with what cannot be heard or seen. I have done this alone and unknown to others. Therefore, I have composed eight stupid poems and written them on the river's rocks.

灌水之陽有溪焉，東流入于瀟水。或曰冉氏嘗居也，故姓是溪為冉溪。或曰可以染也，名之以其能，故謂之染溪。余以愚觸罪，謫瀟水上，愛是溪，入二三里，得其尤絕者家焉。古有愚公谷，今予家是溪，而名莫定，土之居者猶齗齗然，不可以不更也，故更之為愚溪。

愚溪之上，買小丘為愚丘。自愚丘東北行六十步，得泉焉，又買居之，為愚泉。愚泉凡六穴，皆出山下平地，蓋正出也。合流屈曲而南，為愚溝。遂負土累石，塞其隘為愚池。愚池之東為愚堂。其南為愚亭。池之中為愚島。嘉木異石錯置，皆山水之奇者，以余故，咸以愚辱焉。

夫水，智者樂也。今是溪獨見辱於愚，何哉。蓋其流甚下，不可以溉灌。又峻急，多坻石，大舟不可入也。幽邃淺狹，蛟龍不屑，不能興雲雨。無以利世，而適類於余，然則雖辱而愚之，可也。甯武子邦無道則愚。智而為愚者也。顏子終日不違如愚，睿而為愚者也，皆不得為真愚。今余遭有道，而違於理，悖於事，故凡為愚者，莫我若也。夫然，則天下莫能爭是溪，余得專而名焉。

溪雖莫利於世，而善鑒萬類。清瑩秀澈，鏘鳴金石，能使愚者喜笑眷慕，樂而不能去也。余雖不合於俗，亦頗以文墨自慰，漱滌萬物，牢籠百態，而無所避之。以愚辭歌愚溪，則茫然而不違，昏然而同歸，超鴻蒙，混希夷。寂寥而莫我知也。於是作八愚詩，紀于溪石上。

....

Note: The Kuan River is 50 kilometers southwest of Yungchou and mentioned here merely as a geographical referent. A *li* is one-third of a mile or one-half of a kilometer. During the first millenium BC, Mister Stupid's Valley

(Yukungku 愚公谷) was south of Tzupo 淄博 in Shantung province. In the *Analects* (6.21), Confucius is recorded as saying, "The wise delight in water, the kind delight in mountains." Also in the *Analects* (5.20), Confucius says, "As for Ning Wu-tzu, when the Tao prevailed in the realm, he acted wise, when the Tao didn't prevail in the realm, he acted stupid. Others might match his wisdom but not his stupidity." Again, in the *Analects* (2.9) Confucius says, "I have talked with Yen all day, and he has never raised objections, as if he were stupid. But when he leaves, I notice how he acts, and he manifests what I teach. Hui is not stupid." Yen Hui was Confucius's favorite disciple. The eight poems that went with this preface have been lost—or were simply scattered among those that follow. (642)

54. AFTER PLANTING BAMBOO BENEATH THE EAVES
苦簜下始栽竹

I made a thatched roof for my hut
the constant heat sapped my strength
also my legs swelled up
and the humidity didn't help
a neighbor to the east gave me some advice
planting bamboo would make it cool
the very idea made me smile
I carried a shovel to the cliffs to the west
the soil here in Ch'u contains lots of odd rocks
I dug and chiseled until I was exhausted
until the river wind said it was late
fast as I could I hauled everything back
their canes now hum beyond the far shore
and sway beside my shaded front steps
I made an effort to protect the rhizomes
I nourished the shoots with springwater
my windows now stay open at night
I don't use a fan anymore
with the night air also comes dew
my sleeping mat finally feels cool
spiders make webs in the thicket of leaves
birds perch at dawn on the higher branches
I don't know what happened to the noise
my thoughts are quieter now
what a blessing their upright form
they made me give up my hermit plans
they might not include wild vines
or masses of foliage or flowers
and they might not remind me of winter
but why should I say goodbye to mountains

瘴茆葺為宇，溽暑恆侵肌。適有重膇疾，蒸鬱寧所宜。
東鄰幸導我，樹竹邀涼颸。欣然愜吾志，荷鍤西巖垂。
楚壤多怪石，墾鑿力已疲。江風忽云暮，輿曳還相追。
蕭瑟過極浦，旖旎附幽墀。貞根期永固，胎爾寒泉滋。
夜窗遂不掩，羽扇寧復持。清泠集濃露，枕簟凄已知。
網蟲依密葉，曉禽棲迴枝。豈伊紛囂間，重以心慮怡。
嘉爾亭亭質，自遠棄幽期。不見野蔓草，蓊蔚有華姿。
諒無凌寒色，豈與青山辭。

....

NOTE: Written in Yungchou in the summer of 810. Liu moved across the Hsiao to the Yuhsi River in the fifth month of this year. The former location of his hut is now the site of a shrine built by the authorities of Yungchou to honor his memory. Of course, Liu needed a garden, and what's a Chinese garden without some bamboo and strangely shaped rocks. Liu's role model was T'ao Yuan-ming, who chose to live among farmers rather than hermits. (1223)

55. The Overseas Pomegranate I Recently Planted 新植海石榴

Its flimsy stalk isn't more than a foot
I can see it far off in the land of immortals
beside deserted steps beneath a winter moon
or below rose-colored clouds in a distant dream
a rare tree uprooted from fertile soil
a pretty thing replanted in the moss
its color dormant in its noble roots
for whom did it bloom in the past

弱植不盈尺，遠意駐蓬瀛。月寒空堦曙，幽夢綵雲生。
糞壤擢珠樹，莓苔插瓊英。芳根閟顏色，徂歲為誰榮。

....

NOTE: Written in Yungchou in the summer of 810. The pomegranate first arrived in China from Persia via the land route known as the Silk Road. But another variety came from India by ship, and apparently it's this variety that's meant here. The land of immortals was also thought to be in the ocean—overseas. Liu uses the pomegranate here to represent himself—uprooted from the rich cultural centers of the North and transplanted among the hill tribes of the South. (1228)

IX. Cookpot Pool 鈷鉧潭記

Cookpot Pool is west of West Mountain and begins where the Janhsi River comes rushing from the south then turns east when it meets the mountain's rocks. From beginning to end the current is strong and gets stronger as it crashes along and eats away the banks. But because it stops when it finally encounters rocks, it becomes wider and deeper, and the current creates whirlpools, then continues on more slowly. The place where it's clear and calm is surrounded by trees and cascades and amounts to more than an acre or two.

There was someone living above this spot, and because I often visited it, one day the owner knocked on my door. He said, "I can't pay the taxes, and my debts have piled up. Since I've cleared some other land on the mountain and have moved there, I would like to sell the field above the pool to pay off what I owe." I was only too happy to oblige. I then raised the bank and extended the fence and led the spring to a higher place where the sound of the water falling into the pool would be louder. It's an especially fine place for viewing the moon in mid-autumn or for looking at the height of the heavens and the vastness of the firmament.

What else could cause me to enjoy living among hill tribes and to forget about my old home if not this pool?

鼓鉧潭在西山西，其始蓋冉水自南奔注，抵山石，屈折東流。其顛委勢峻，盪擊益暴，齧其涯，故旁廣而中深，畢至石乃止，流沫成輪，然後徐行。其清而平者且十畝餘，有樹環焉，有泉懸焉。

其上有居者，以予之亟游也，一旦款門來告曰，不勝官租私卷之委積，既芟山而更居，願以潭上田貿財以緩禍。予樂而如其言。則崇其臺，延其檻，行其泉於高者而墮之潭，有聲潨然。尤與中秋觀月為宜，於以見天之高，氣之迥。

孰使予樂居夷而忘故土者，非茲潭也歟。(764)

X. The Little Hill West of Cookpot Pool
鈷鉧潭西小丘記

Eight days after reaching West Mountain, I followed a trail from the base of the mountain northwest 200 paces and arrived at Cookpot Pool again. Twenty-five paces farther west, there was a fish weir where the current was strong and deep. Above the weir there was a hill covered with trees and bamboo. Sticking out of the earth, as if angry or arrogant and competing over which had the oddest shape, were too many rocks to count. Those sticking out and bending down looked like horses or oxen drinking from a stream. Those lunging forward and standing up looked like bears climbing a mountain.

The hill was so small, it couldn't have been a tenth of an acre and could have fit inside a cage. When I asked who owned it, someone said the T'ang family had stopped farming it, and it was for sale, but no one had bought it. When I asked how much, I was told it was only 400 coins, and I was happy to buy it. When Li Shen-yuan and Yuan K'e-chi went there with me, they were delighted, finding it beyond their expectations. We then got some tools and cut the weeds and removed the dead trees and burned the debris. Suddenly the beautiful trees and bamboo and strangely shaped rocks all stood out. Looking around at the soaring mountain, the floating clouds, the flowing stream, the birds and animals at play, we saw how each happily contributed its skill and talent in service of this hill. As we lay down on our mats, cool shapes filled our eyes, babbling sounds filled our ears, a vast emptiness filled our spirits, and an utter stillness filled our hearts. Having acquired two such special places in less than ten days, I doubted even those who loved such things in the past ever achieved something this special.

Indeed, if the splendors of this hill were transported to the ancient capitals in the North, those who value landscapes would have fought with each other to buy it, with the price going up a thousand pieces of gold a day until it would have been beyond anyone's reach. And here it is in this prefecture, abandoned, ignored, and looked down upon by farmers and fishermen, and costing a mere 400 coins—and on the market for years. And now Shen-yuan, K'e-chi, and I have happily acquired it for ourselves.

Is this not a happy result? Hence, I've written this on a rock to congratulate this hill on its good fortune.

得西山後八日，尋山口西北道二百步，又得鈷鉧潭。潭西二十五步，當湍而浚者為魚梁。梁之上有丘焉，生竹樹。其石之突怒偃蹇，負土而出，爭為奇狀者，殆不可數。其嶔然相累而下者，若牛馬之飲于溪，其衝然角列而上者，若熊羆之登于山。

丘之小不能一畝，可以籠而有之。問其主，曰唐氏之棄地，貨而不售。問其價，曰止四百。余憐而售之。李深源，元克己時同遊，皆大喜，出自意外。即更取器用，剷刈穢草，伐去惡木，烈火而焚之。嘉木立，美竹露，奇石顯。由其中以望，則山之高，雲之浮，溪之流，鳥獸之遨遊，舉熙熙然廻巧獻技，以效茲丘之下。枕席而臥，則清泠之狀與目謀，瀯瀯之聲與耳謀，悠然而虛者與神謀，淵然而靜者與心謀。不匝旬而得異地者二，雖古好事之士，或未能至焉。

噫，以茲丘之勝，致之灃鎬鄠杜，則貴游之士爭買者，日增千金而愈不可得。今棄是州也，農夫漁夫過而陋之，賈四百，連歲不能售。而我與深源克己獨喜得之，是其果有遭乎。書於石，所以賀茲丘之遭也。 (765)

XI. Going to the Little Rock Pond West of Little Hill 至小丘西小石潭記

Walking 120 paces west from Little Hill, beyond a stand of bamboo, I heard the sound of water chiming like jade pendants or earrings and was captivated. After clearing a path through the bamboo, I looked down to find a small pond. The water was exceptionally clear, and the bottom was completely lined with rocks. Those barely sticking out near the banks were shaped like islands or mountains, cliffs or crags. Bright green vines entwined around the dark branches of the trees and dangled down at random. There must have been a hundred fish in the pond, swimming as if supported by nothing but air. As the sunlight shone through, their shadows formed patterns on the rocks. They were perfectly still, then suddenly they were somewhere else, darting back and forth, as if they were playing with this visitor.

To the southwest, the pond curved like a dipper or a snake and wasn't fully visible. The bank was jagged like dog teeth, and I couldn't see where the water was coming from. As I sat above the pond, I was surrounded on all sides by trees and bamboo. It was so quiet and deserted, I felt a chill and started to feel anxious. The place was too secluded for me, and I didn't stay long. I wrote this and left.

My companions on that excursion included Wu Wu-ling, Kung-ku, and my cousin, Tsung-hsuan. Shu-chi and Feng-yi, two young boys of the Ts'ui family, served as our attendants.

從小丘西行百二十步，隔篁竹，聞水聲，如鳴珮環，心樂之。伐竹取道，下見小潭。水尤清冽，全石以為底。近岸卷石底以出，為坻為嶼，為嵁為巖。青樹翠蔓，蒙絡搖綴，參差披拂。潭中魚可百許頭，皆若空遊無所依。日光下澈，影布石上，怡然不動，俶爾遠逝，往來翕忽，似與遊者相樂。

潭西南而望，斗折蛇行，明滅可見。其岸勢犬牙差互，不可知其源。坐潭上，四面竹樹環合。寂寥無人，淒神寒骨，悄愴幽邃。以其境過清，不可久居。乃記之而去。

同遊者，吳武陵，龔古，余弟宗玄。隸而從者，崔氏二小生，曰恕己，曰奉壹。

NOTE: Wu Wu-ling also appears in poems 37 and 75 and was a constant companion between 808 and 812. Kung-ku was one of Liu's friends, but I can't find anything more about him. (Liu) Tsung-hsuan was Liu's cousin on his father's side and accompanied him to Yungchou. (767)

56. Taking a Morning Walk Alone to the Pond North of the Yuhsi after It Rained
雨後曉行獨至愚溪北池

Sandbars free of overnight clouds
village walls lit by the morning sun
a pristine pond encircled by trees
last night's rain scattered by the wind
happy having nothing to do
my mind becomes one with all this

宿雲散洲渚，曉日明村塢。高樹臨清池，風驚夜來雨。
予心適無事，偶此成賓主。

....

NOTE: Written in Yungchou in the summer of 810. Liu built his hermitage about 500 meters upstream from where the waters of the Yuhsi merged with those of the Hsiao. According to Liu's journals, North Pond, which he also called Yuchih Pond, was sixty paces northwest of his house. The pond is now little more than a weed-choked spring. (1217)

57. Accompanying Hermit Hsieh to Yuchih Pond at Dawn 旦攜謝山人至愚池

After bathing I put on a light hat
at dawn the pond air felt cool
I prefer the world beyond the dust
especially out walking with a hermit
as the clouds disappeared hills filled the distance
a few geese called high above
officials can keep their clever ways
I'd rather be back in Fu Hsi's times

新沐換輕幘，曉池風露清。自諧塵外意，況與幽人行。
霞散衆山迴，天高數雁鳴。機心付當路，聯適羲皇情。

....

NOTE: Written in Yungchou in the summer of 810. Geese supposedly didn't fly south of the Hengshan Mountains, the southernmost peak of which was 150 kilometers to the north. Given that it's summer, these geese must be lost. Yuchih Pond was less than a minute's walk north of Liu's house. A stiffer more formal hat was worn while performing public duties—not that Liu had much to do in that regard. The age during which China's legendary emperors such as Fu Hsi ruled was considered a time when natural ways prevailed. (1211)

58. Inspecting the Yuhsi after an Early Summer Rain 夏初雨後尋愚溪

After a long rain the sky finally cleared
I followed the river's winding shore
testing overgrown springs with my staff
tying back new bamboo with my sash
why do I mutter so much
I want to be alone I guess
thanks to my freedom from running errands
I can sing and stay still when it's hot

悠悠雨初霽，獨繞清溪曲。引杖試荒泉，解帶圍新竹。
沉吟亦何事，寂寞固所欲。幸此息營營，嘯歌靜炎燠。

....

NOTE: Written in Yungchou in the summer of 810. The penultimate line is sarcastic. The post to which Liu was assigned came with no real duties—hence his residence on a minor tributary beyond the west shore of the Hsiao, across from the town where he was appointed deputy magistrate. Three years after Liu died, a monk visited Liu's former residence and wrote Liu Yu-hsi that it was no longer what it was. Saddened by the monk's report, Yu-hsi composed three poems titled "Yuhsi Lament" 傷愚溪. (1213)

YUHSI LAMENT 傷愚溪 BY LIU YU-HSI

ONE

The river flows on and spring keeps returning
the thatched hut is vacant but the swallows are back
there's nothing but a courtyard of weeds beyond the screen
and a pomegranate tree in bloom as usual

溪水悠悠春自來，草堂無主燕飛回。隔簾唯見中庭草，一樹山榴依舊開。

Two

Traces of his calligraphy still grace a crumbling wall
his grove of tree servants belongs to a neighbor now
coming through the village gate built in his honor
all I see is a woodcutter's cart in the last rays of sunset

草聖數行留壞壁，木奴千樹屬鄰家。唯見里門通德榜，殘陽寂寞出樵車。

Three

Liu's gate and the bamboo-lined lane are still there
and more moss and weeds every day
even if the neighbor knew how to play a flute
friends from Shanyang don't visit anymore

柳門竹巷依依在，野草青苔日日多。縱有鄰人解吹笛，山陽舊侶更誰過。

....

Two: An impoverished man once planted orange trees and told his family one day they would make them rich. They laughed, but he turned out to be right. The story also appears in poem 136. Liu planted hundreds of orange trees in Yungchou as well as in Liuchou.

Three: Hearing a neighbor playing a flute, Hsiang Hsiu 向秀 wrote a poem about the death of Chi K'ang 嵇康, one of his fellow Seven Sages of the Bamboo Grove. The bamboo grove where these famous would-be recluses lived when they weren't at court was located in Shanyang county, north of Loyang. (1214)

59. RIVERSIDE HOME 溪居

I'd grown tired of court attire
this rustication among hill tribes was welcome
with nothing to do and farmers for neighbors
sometimes I feel like a hermit
at dawn tilling dew-covered grass
at dusk banging oars on river rocks
not meeting anyone coming or going
I sing out loud beneath the blue southern sky

久為簪組累，幸此南夷謫。閑依農圃鄰，偶似山林客。
曉耕翻露草，夜榜響溪石。來往不逢人，長歌楚天碧。

....

NOTE: Written in Yungchou in the fall of 810. The Yuhsi was narrow in places
and lined with boulders—hence "banging oars on river rocks." (1213)

60. Miscellany Presented in Reply to Scholar Lou About to Leave for Huainan
酬婁秀才將之淮南見贈之什

I was sent far away to enjoy life alone
who would have guessed I would meet an old friend
taking pity on broken wings with kind words
soothing ragged fins with life-saving water
our feelings as colleagues haven't changed
but the joys of companionship are new
wandering without a goal wasting time
immune to the pains of spring dancing drunk
even if the pleasures of wind and moon have ceased
the stars and frost we've shared has brought us closer
treating fame as a calamity
we chose the Tao for our neighbor
our schemes were roof tiles in a storm
our suspicions simply misperceptions
wearing an official's hat I still write poems
despite your poverty you still carry a sword
suddenly the season seems late
suddenly our parting is today
this happy time won't come again
what is it that's dragging you off
my spirit is leaving with you on the river
I'll have to console my shadow on this side of Heaven
what can I do on that stream to the west
what can I do alone but go fishing

遠棄甘幽獨，誰言值故人。好音憐鎩羽，濡沫慰窮鱗。
同志情惟舊，相知樂更新。浪遊輕費日，醉舞詎傷春。
風月歡寧間，星霜分益親。已將名是患，還用道為鄰。
機事齊飄瓦，嫌猜比拾塵。高冠余肯賦，長鋏子忘貧。
晼晚驚移律，睽攜忽此辰。開顏時不再，絆足去何因。
海上銷魂別，天邊弔影身。祇應西澗水，寂寞但垂綸。

....

NOTE: Written in Yungchou in the fall of 810. Lou T'u-nan 婁圖南 was a great-grandson of Lou Shih-te 婁師德, a director of the Chancellery in the early T'ang. Despite his esteemed ancestor, Lou turned his back on the prospect of a career as an official. He decided instead on the path of an educated vagabond and was visiting Buddhist and Taoist masters in South China. Hence, he held no post and is simply called a "scholar" here. Lou followed Liu to Yungchou in 806, the year after Liu arrived, and over the next three years the two became inseparable companions. The area to which Lou is now traveling, Huainan, includes the land immediately north of the middle reaches of the Yangtze. The image in the fourth line of two fish trying to survive in a wheel rut by squirting water on each other is from *Chuangtzu* 6.5. As for the official's hat Liu wears despite having no duties, and the sword Lou carries despite having no assignment, both lines are paraphrased from the beginning of Ch'u Yuan's "Crossing the River" 涉江, where they represent the resolutions of youth undiminished by age or unfavorable circumstance. The "stream to the west" would be the Yuhsi, where Liu moved earlier that year. I've gone along with the variant 同志 *t'ung-chih* (colleague) in line five in place of 困志 *k'un-chih* (troubled intention). (1131)

61. On Hearing about the Field-Plowing Ceremony 聞籍田有感

Before long our lord's chariot will reach that royal field
I'm stuck in Changsha and another year is over
no one in the palace knows how to talk to gods
where in the capital can I send a letter

天田不日降皇輿，留滯長沙歲又除。宣室無由問釐事，周南何處託成書。

....

NOTE: Written in Yungchou in the winter of 810. Despite committing himself to the life of a semi-recluse, Liu sees a chance—mirage though it is—to return to court. In the tenth month of that year, Emperor Hsien-tsung announced he would conduct a ceremony in the eastern suburbs of Ch'ang-an the following spring to ensure better harvests. It was an expensive ceremony and rarely performed, and Liu wishes he could be involved as an adviser. As a result of drought and warfare, however, the ceremony was canceled. In the second line, Liu substitutes the Han-dynasty poet Chia Yi 賈誼 for himself. Chia was also banished to the Hsiang River—but to Changsha, not Yungchou—and likewise wished he could take part in a ceremony the emperor planned to conduct, in his case at the sacred mountain of Taishan 泰山. However, before the emperor banished Chia, he had the foresight to ask him about the proper way to deal with the gods. (1243)

62. Getting Up at Midnight to Gaze at West Garden Just as the Moon Was Rising
中夜起望西園值月上

Awakened by the sound of dripping dew
I opened the door to West Garden
the winter moon was rising from East Ridge
turning the bamboo pale white
the waterfall upstream sounded louder
now and then I heard a bird cry
I leaned against a pillar until dawn
wondering how to put such solitude into words

覺聞繁露墜，開戶臨西園。寒月上東嶺，泠泠疏竹根。
石泉遠逾響，山鳥時一喧。倚楹遂至旦，寂寞將何言。

. . . .

NOTE: Written in Yungchou in the winter of 810. East Ridge refers to the combined ridges of East Mountain and Chienchiuling on the east shore of the Hsiao River, where Liu lived during his first five years in Yungchou. The Yuhsi was marked by a number of cascades upstream from Liu's new residence beyond the Hsiao's west shore. (1217)

63. Living out of Town at the End of the Year 郊居歲暮

Living in seclusion near a mountain village
I'm surprised to be on my own at year-end
a woodcutter's song drifts in from the wilds
ashes from a fire settle in my yard
worldly distractions have become more distant
pleasures too have waned with the year
I consider in silence why this is so
but why compare the present with the past

屏居負山郭，歲暮驚離索。野迥樵唱來，庭空燒燼落。
世紛因事遠，心賞隨年薄。默默諒何為，徒成今與昨。

....

NOTE: Written in Yungchou in the winter of 810. In China, the end of one year and beginning of the next is a time when friends and relatives visit each other and celebrate their longevity. Most of Liu's friends were on the east shore. An uncle who had lived south of him on the west shore died earlier that year, and a cousin had left the previous year. Also, this was Liu's first winter on his own. He spent the previous five at Lunghsing Monastery. (1216)

64. Musing about the Peony below the Steps 戲題堦前芍藥

When others have faded with the season
this gorgeous bloom decorates the dawn
its bright red petals drunk with dew
coquettishly detaining the spring
enjoying the sun by itself until dusk
swaying in a summer breeze
at night through the window its perfume floods in
lying in the dark I know someone loves me
having sent this gift from the Ch'en and Wei rivers
to this person in the far distant South

凡卉與時謝，妍華麗茲晨。歆紅醉濃露，窈窕留餘春。
孤賞白日暮，暄風動搖頻。夜窗藹芳氣，幽臥知相親。
願致溱洧贈，悠悠南國人。

....

NOTE: Written in Yungchou in the early summer of 811. The original home
of the peony was in the area between the Ch'en and Wei Rivers in the Yellow
River watershed of Honan province. Boys and girls there used the flower as
a token of love, as in the poem "The Ch'en and Wei" in the Book of Poetry.
Liu's wife died prior to his exile, and he didn't remarry until his subsequent
exile to Liuchou. He did, however, take a concubine around this time. But this
peony must have been sent by someone else, most likely a male friend. (1229)

65. Walking to the Ferry after It Rained 雨晴至江渡

When the rain finally stopped I decided to stretch my legs
I headed for the ferry before the sun could set
as the water level dropped the ferry path appeared
hanging in the trees was storm debris

江雨初晴思遠步，日西獨向愚溪渡。渡頭水落村逕成，撩亂浮槎在高樹。

....

NOTE: Written in Yungchou in the summer of 811. One of the ferries that connected the east and west banks of the Hsiao was at the mouth of the Yuhsi River, several hundred meters downstream from where Liu was living. The precipitous drop in the water level was along the Yuhsi, not the Hsiao. Some commentators think the storm debris was the remains of Stupid Pavilion Liu built the previous summer near Stupid Pond, just north of his Stupid House. (1220)

66. Passing Through a Deserted Village on an Autumn Morning Walk to South Valley
秋曉行南谷經荒村

At the end of autumn after a heavy frost
I set off early for a secluded valley
the bridge was covered with yellow leaves
nothing remained of the village but old trees
except for a few hardy flowers it was bleak
overgrown springs gurgled faintly
having given up schemes long ago
I wonder why I frightened the deer

杪秋霜露重，晨起行幽谷。黃葉覆溪橋，荒村唯古木。
寒花疏寂歷，幽泉微斷續。機心久已忘，何事驚麋鹿。

....

NOTE: Written in Yungchou in the late fall of 811. South Valley was the location of two of Liu's favorite spots: Rock Creek 石澗 and Rock Channel 石渠, both of which were immortalized in his travel journals. The valley was 2 kilometers south of his hermitage on the Yuhsi. The reference of the last couplet is to a pair of Taoist stories. In the first (*Chuangtzu* 12.11), a disciple of Confucius tries to convince a farmer to use a device to make irrigation easier, and the farmer scoffs that such a device would be injurious to his ability to act according to the Tao. In the second (*Liehtzu* 2.13), a fisherman who was followed by gulls on his daily walks along the beach was urged to try catching one of them. When he did, the gulls no longer came near him. (1217)

67. WITH LIU TWENTY-EIGHT MOURNING LU OF HENGCHOU: SENT TO CENSORS LI AND YUAN IN CHIANGLING 同劉二十八哭呂衡州兼寄江陵李元二侍御

Hengshan's Pillar of Heaven recently collapsed
his colleagues look forlorn and we cry when we meet
hopefully what he wrote is recorded on bamboo
his name isn't likely to appear on any bell
he leaves an empty shack and an acre of land
and a grave mound as big as a shrine hall
I wish I could talk with our distant Chiangling friends
every time I sigh about Yuan-lung at night

衡岳新摧天柱峰，士林頫頷泣相逢。祇令文字傳青簡，不使功名上景鍾。
三畝空留懸磬室，九原猶寄若堂封。遙想荊州人物論，幾回中夜惜元龍。

....

NOTE: Written in Yungchou in the winter of 811. Liu Twenty-Eight refers
to the poet's friend Liu Yu-hsi, who ranked twenty-eighth in his generation
in his clan by birth. Yu-hsi was serving as magistrate of Langchou (modern
Changte 常德), 300 kilometers to the north. Exile normally included restric-
tions on travel outside the place of exile, but if "with" in the title means "at the
same location" rather than "joining," then Yu-hsi apparently found a way. Li
Ching-lien 李景儉 and Yuan Chen 元稹 were serving in Chiangling, or Ching-
chou 荊州, in the middle reaches of the Yangtze. Their fellow reformer and
banished friend, Lu Wen 呂溫, died at the age of forty in the autum of 811 in
Hengchou (Hengyang)—hence his name here: Lu of Hengchou. Lu was one of
Liu's closest friends. They both served together at court. Liu compares him to
one of the more famous peaks of Hengshan just north of Hengchou: Tienchu,
or Pillar of Heaven. Important texts were written on strips of bamboo that
were tied together to form a book. Bronze bells were cast at great expense
and rarely included the names of anyone but their owners. For some reason,
Lu's body didn't make it back to the family cemetery in North China but got
only as far as Chiangling, where Liu's other friends apparently had something

to do with its burial. The reference in the last line is to one of the heroes of the Later Han dynasty, Ch'en Teng 陳登 (169–207 BC), whose sobriquet was Yuan-lung. Like their friend, he died young, at the age of thirty-nine. Liu Tsung-yuan was himself going on thirty-nine when he wrote this. (1155)

68. Occasional Poem on a Summer Day 夏晝偶作

Here in the South it's so hot I feel drunk
after dozing on a bench I opened the north window
it was noon and I couldn't hear any other sound
just a farm boy pounding tea beyond the bamboo

南州溽暑醉如酒，隱机熟眠開北牖。日午獨覺無餘聲，山童隔竹敲茶臼。

....

NOTE: Written in Yungchou in the summer of 812. During the T'ang dynasty, one of the most common ways of processing tea leaves was to pound them in a mortar after they had been oxidized by a brief exposure to heat from the sun or in a wok. The resulting powder was then whisked with boiling water and drunk. This process has remained in vogue in Japan but more or less disappeared in China 500 years ago. (1220)

69. FISHERMAN 漁翁

A fisherman spent the night beside West Cliff
he drew water from the river and made a bamboo fire at dawn
when the fog finally lifted he was gone
hi-ho echoed through a green world
in the middle of the river he looked back at the sky
the cliff's mindless clouds were right behind him

漁翁夜傍西巖宿，曉汲清湘燃楚竹。煙銷日出不見人，欸乃一聲山水綠。
迴看天際下中流，巖上無心雲相逐。

....

NOTE: Written in Yungchou in the seventh month of 812. I suspect it was
about this time that Liu moved his residence, if he hadn't done so earlier,
to the area near the mouth of the Yuhsi. Had he not been living there, he
wouldn't have seen the events described in this poem. Being on the west
shore of the Hsiao, Chaoyang Cliff was sometimes referred to as West Cliff.
The fourth line has given rise to considerable ink by commentators. Does
"ai-nai" (or "ai-ao" as it was pronounced in the T'ang) refer to the slap of the
fisherman's oars, or does it refer to one of the five songs of that title by the
T'ang poet Yuan Chieh (723–772)? While Yuan was traveling up the Hsiang
to his post, which was the next major town past Yungchou (or Lingling), he
composed five extempore songs for the trackers to chant while they were
hauling his boat upstream and titled them "Ai-ao," or "Hi-ho," as in *Snow
White and the Seven Dwarfs*. Yuan Chieh was a forerunner of the "ancient
text" style made famous by Liu Tsung-yuan, and his songs would have been
well known to Liu. If the second interpretation is correct, I'm thinking he
heard the fourth of those five songs: "North of Lingling where the Hsiang
flows east / the wonders of Wu Creek fill the shore / the tumbled rocks at its
mouth are worth your time / who'll join me there for some fishing?" 零陵郡北
湘水東，浯溪形勝滿湘中. 溪口石顛堪自逸, 誰能相伴作漁翁. In the fourth line of
Liu's poem, some editions have *lu* 淥 (clear) instead of *lu* 綠 (green). The same
pair of variants also appear in poems 31 and 74. (1252)

70. WRITTEN AT SOUTH CREEK 南澗中題

Autumn air reached South Creek before me
I hiked here alone at noon
a swirling wind rattled the leaves
the shade kept changing shape
as soon as I arrived I felt blessed
before long I forgot my fatigue
a lost bird singing in a secluded valley
winter algae dancing in the ripples
my spirit left me when I was banished
my tears for those I love are no use
living alone I'm easily moved
losing my way seldom helps
what is this depression about
this quandry I know too well
who will come here in the future
and experience what I feel

秋氣集南澗，獨遊亭午時。迴風一蕭瑟，林影久參差。
始至若有得，稍深遂忘疲。羈禽響幽谷，寒藻舞淪漪。
去國魂已游，懷人淚空垂。孤生易為感，失路少所宜。
索寞竟何事，徘徊祇自知。誰為後來者，當與此心期。

....

NOTE: Written in Yungchou in the seventh month of 812 at the same time
as the previous poem. This was when Liu wrote his famous journals about
the area south of his second Yuhsi residence, in which he calls South Creek
"Rock Creek." The creek joined the Hsiao across from Yungchou's Taiping
Gate, the city's southernmost gate. The "lost bird" and "winter algae" are
self-references, recalling Liu's isolation and rootlessness. His tears are for
his uncle, Ts'ui Min, who died in Yungchou in 810, and for his cousin Lu
Tsun, who accompanied him to Yungchou but left on an assignment in 809.
Lu eventually returned, but not until after this poem was written. While

they were in Yungchou, Ts'ui and Lu both lived near South Creek. In the ninth line, I've read *you* 游 (leave, travel) as a stand-in for *shih* 逝 (depart, die), which is the character used by Ch'u Yuan and others in nearly identical lines. (1192)

XII. Yuan Tributary 袁家渴記

Going southwest by boat on the Janhsi River for 10 *li* [5 kilometers], there are five scenic places, but none like Cookpot Pool. Going west from the mouth of the river on foot, there are eight or nine, but none like West Mountain. Going southeast from Chaoyang Cliff by boat as far as the Wu River, there are three, but none like Yuan Tributary. These are Yungchou's most idyllic and unusual places.

In the dialects of the South, people call waterways that are branches "tributaries," which they pronounce *ho* [coarse cloth] as in *yi-ho* [coarse clothing]. The upper section of this particular tributary merges with the ridges of South Lodge. The lower section merges with Hundred Family Shoals. In between are a number of sandbars, small brooks, clear pools, and rapids, as it wends this way, then that. Where the current is calm, the water is dark black. Where it's strong, it's a frothy white. As I traveled it by boat, it appeared to end, then suddenly it opened up again. A small hill rises out of the water and is covered with beautiful rocks and vegetation that remains green year-round. Its slopes include a number of caverns, and there are lots of white pebbles at its base. Among the trees are maple, laurel, rhododendron, mahogany, oak, cedar, camphor, and pomelo, and the plants include orchids and angelica. There is also an unusual kind of mimosa that grows like a vine and wraps around waterside rocks. When the wind blows down from the surrounding mountains, it shakes the great trees and flattens the plants, scattering their flowers and leaves and their myriad scents, and it whips up waves and whirlpools and blows them back upstream, and whether something is blown apart or flourishes depends on the season. This is how it generally looks, but I lack the words to describe it completely.

The people of Yungchou don't frequent this place. Having discovered it, I don't dare keep it to myself and am making it known to the world. Since the Yuan family own the land, this is the name I've used.

由冉溪西南水行十里，山水之可取者五，莫若鈷鉧潭。由溪口而西，陸行，可取者八九，莫若西山。由朝陽巖東南水行，至蕪江，可取者三，莫若袁家渴。皆永中幽麗奇處也。

　楚越之間方言，謂水之支流者為渴。音若衣褐之褐。渴上與南館高嶂合，下與百家瀨合。其中重洲小溪，澄潭淺渚，間廁曲折。平者深黑，峻者沸白。舟行若窮，忽又無際。有小山出水中，皆美石，上生青叢，冬夏常蔚然。其旁多巖洞，其下多白礫。其樹多楓柟石楠梗櫧樟柚，草則蘭芝。又有異卉，類合歡而蔓生，轇轕水石。每風自四山而下，振動大木，掩苒眾草，紛紅駭綠，蓊葧香氣，衝濤旋瀨，退貯谿谷，搖颺葳蕤，與時推移。其大都如此，余無以窮其狀。

　　永之人未嘗遊焉，余得之不敢專也，出而傳於世。其地主袁氏，故以名焉。

....

NOTE: This and the following two prose pieces were written around the same time as the two previous poems, in the fall of 812. (768)

XIII. ROCK CHANNEL 石渠記

Walking southwest from the tributary, after less than a hundred paces I came to a rock-lined channel across which people had built a bridge. I could hear a spring babbling, first loud then faint. The width of the channel was maybe a foot, or possibly two, and its length was ten or so paces. Where the current met a boulder, it went below it. I continued past the boulder and came to a rock pool covered by calamus grass and lined by green moss. As the current turned west again, it went below a cliff then dropped into a small pond to the north. The pond was less than a hundred feet in area, and it was clear and deep, and there were lots of minnows. As I followed its course northward, I had an unobstructed view of where it finally flowed into the [Yuan] tributary. Along its banks were unusual rocks and trees and plants, including arrow bamboo. It was a perfect place to sit and relax. The wind shook the treetops and echoed among the cliffs. I watched in silence, listening to sounds from far away.

After the magistrate of Yungchou first led me here, I removed the deadfall, cleared away the dirt and rocks, piled everything up and burned it so the channel would have more room. Unfortunately, no one has ever written about this place, hence I have taken the trouble to make a record of what is here to pass on to others and have inscribed it in a sunny spot so that those with such interests who come looking for it in the future can find it more easily. On the eighth day of the first month in the seventh year of the Yuanho period [812], I dredged the channel as far as the boulder. On the nineteenth day of the tenth month, I continued past the boulder to the rock pool and the small pond. This ends my description of the channel's attractions.

渴西南行，不能百步，得石渠，民橋其上。有泉幽幽然，其鳴乍大乍細。渠之廣，或咫尺，或倍尺，其長可十許步。其流抵大石，伏出其下。踰石而往，有石泓，昌蒲被之，青鮮環周。又折西行，旁陷巖石下，北墮小潭。潭幅員減百尺，清深多儵魚。又北曲行紆餘，睨若無窮，然卒入于渴。其側皆詭石怪木，奇卉美箭。可列坐而庥焉。風搖其顛，韻動崖谷。視之既靜，其聽始遠。

予從州牧得之，攬去翳朽，決疏土石，既崇而焚，既釃而盈。惜其未始有傳焉者，故累記其所屬，遺之其人，書之其陽，俾後好事者求之得以易。元和七年正月八日，蠲渠至大石。十月十九日，踰石得石泓小潭。渠之美於是始窮也。（770）

XIV. Rock Creek 石澗記

Once I finished with Rock Channel, I crossed the bridge then went north-west and came down the north side of a dirt hill where people had built another bridge. The stream there was three times wider than Rock Channel. The bottom consisted of a series of rocks that extended to both banks. It resembled a bed or a hallway, or a rolled-out mat, or the threshold to an inner chamber. As the water spread across the rocks, the current looked like lines of weaving and made a sound like a zither. Lifting my robe and wading on, I broke off some arrow bamboo and swept away the old leaves and pushed the dead limbs aside and was able to clear space for eighteen or nineteen folding chairs. The rippling current and sound of splashing water were below, and kingfisher-green trees and dragon-scale rocks provided shade from above. Did people in the past ever enjoy this place? Or will people in the future be able to retrace my steps? I discovered it the same day as Rock Channel.

Coming from the tributary, you reach Rock Channel first, then Rock Creek, while coming from Hundred Family Shoals, you reach Rock Creek first, then Rock Channel. The part of the creek that can be explored leads southeast from Rock Wall Village and includes several delightful spots. As the path continues deeper into the forest and up the mountain, it becomes steeper and more dangerous and too narrow to explore.

石渠之事既窮，上由橋西北，下土山之陰，民又橋焉。其水之大，倍石渠三之一。亙石為底，達于兩涯。若床若堂，若陳筵席，若限閾奧。水平布其上，流若織文，響若操琴。揭跣而往，折竹箭，掃陳葉，排腐木，可羅胡牀十八九居之。交絡之流，觸激之音，皆在牀下，翠羽之木，龍鱗之石，均蔭其上。古之人其有樂乎此邪。後之來者有能追予之踐履邪。得意之日，與石渠同。

由渴而來者，先石渠，後石澗，由百家瀬上而來者，先石澗，後石渠。澗之可窮者，皆出石城村東南，其間可樂者數焉。其上深山幽林，逾峭險，道狹不可窮也。

....

NOTE: The mention of "folding chairs" is curious. Commentators are silent on the subject, but I'm assuming no actual chairs were involved and that this was simply a way of measuring an area, just as floorspace in Taiwan was once measured in tatamis (3' × 6' straw mats). (771)

71. Climbing West Mountain with Ts'ui Ts'e
與崔策登西山

Except for a crane the mountain was silent
it was a dewy autumn river dawn
we crossed a rickety bridge arm in arm
then zigzagged our way above the treetops
from the west peak we looked out as far as we could
the minutest detail was clear
the multiple ridges of Chiuyishan
the tiny outline of Tungting Lake
the farthest limits of heaven and earth
everything in the world stood out
sunlight rippling on disappearing waves
wind-bent weather-beaten bamboo
will I ever get used to this exile
the boredom and utter despair
inheriting the life of a convict
the life span of the oldest-known man
worrying about missteps and stumbles
fearing what I don't know or see
not letting those I love go
not knowing why my heart trembles
disappearing with you among mountains and rivers
happy watching fishes and birds
I'm glad you've agreed to stay longer
it eases the heartache I feel

鶴鳴楚山靜，露白秋江曉。連袂渡危橋，縈迴出林杪。
西岑極遠目，毫末皆可了。重疊九疑高，微茫洞庭小。
迴窮兩儀際，高出萬象表。馳景泛頹波，遙風遞寒篠。
謫居安所習，稍厭從紛擾。生同胥靡遺，壽等彭鏗夭。
蹇連困顛踣，愚蒙怯幽眇。非令親愛疏，誰使心神悄。
偶茲遁山水，得以觀魚鳥。吾子幸淹留，緩我愁腸繞。

NOTE: Written in Yungchou in the fall of 812. Ts'ui Ts'e was the younger brother of Ts'ui Chien 崔簡, who married Liu's older sister—both sisters died before Liu left Ch'ang-an. West Mountain was a few hundred meters northwest of Liu's home on the Yuhsi River—not to be confused with the hill to the southwest currently called West Mountain. Liu called this hill West Mountain because when he first noticed it, it was directly across the Hsiao River from East Mountain. In 2017, I visited the top of the mountain with some local scholars and discovered someone had turned it into a garbage dump. It was a clear day, but we didn't stay long enough to find out whether we could see Chiuyi Mountain or Tungting Lake. Liu's records of his first excursion here in 809 and his subsequent visit in 812 to the rock formation on the west flank of the mountain follow. (1195)

XV. First Visit to West Mountain 始得西山宴游記

Ever since I was disgraced and assigned to this district, I've been living in constant fear. Whenever I've had a chance, I've walked and wandered without aim. With like-minded friends, I've hiked up mountains and through forests and along winding streams to hidden springs and fantastic rock formations. No destination has been beyond our reach. And once we reached our destination, we would flatten the grass and sit down and drain our jugs until we were drunk. And once we were drunk, we would use each other for pillows and fall asleep. And once we were asleep, we would dream. And whatever far-off thoughts we might have previously had, that was what we would dream about. And once we awoke, we would get up. And once we got up, we would go home. I thought I had seen every scenic wonder in the district, but I didn't yet know how extraordinary West Mountain would be.

This year on the twenty-eighth day of the ninth month, while sitting beneath Fahua Monastery's West Pavilion, I gazed at the mountain to the west and suddenly realized it looked different. I summoned my attendants, and we crossed the Hsiang and followed the Janhsi River [the Yuhsi] upstream. We hacked our way through the undergrowth and burned the tall grass until we reached the highest part of the mountain. After pulling ourselves up, we sat down and stretched out our legs. The land of several districts lay below us. The soaring heights and disappearing hollows of the terrain were like so many anthills and crevices in the earth. A thousand *li* seemed a mere arm's length away. Compressed into small piles, nothing was hidden: undulating green hills and winding white waters merged with the sky. In every direction it was the same. It was then that I realized this mountain was special and not just another pile of dirt. It was one with the endless firmament and seemingly without limits, one with all of creation and apparently without end. Lifting a jug, we filled our cups and were soon drunk. Oblivious to the setting sun, we watched the darkness of evening approach from the far horizon until we couldn't see a thing, and still we refused to leave. Our minds were so transfixed, and our bodies so relaxed, we became one with the myriad transformations. Later I realized I had not yet begun to travel, that my travels were just beginning. Hence I wrote this record in the fourth year of the Yuanho period [809].

自余為僇人，居是州，恆惴慄。其隟也，則施施而行，漫漫而游。日與其徒上高山，入深林，窮廻谿，幽泉怪石，無遠不到。到則披草而坐，傾壺而醉。醉則更相枕而臥，臥而夢。意有所極，夢亦同趣。覺而起，起而歸。以為凡是州之山水有異態者，皆我有也，而未始知西山之怪特。

今年九月二十八日，因坐法華西亭，望西山，始指異之。遂命僕人過湘江，緣染溪，斫榛莽，焚茅茷，窮山之高而止。攀援而登，箕踞而遨，則凡數州之土壤，皆在衽席之下。其高下之勢，岈然洼然，若垤若穴，尺寸千里，攢蹙累積，莫得遯隱。縈青繚白，外與天際，四望如一。然後知是山之特立，不與培塿為類，悠悠乎與顥氣俱，而莫得其涯，洋洋乎與造物者游，而不知其所窮。引觴滿酌，頹然就醉，不知日之入。蒼然暮色，自遠而至，至無所見，而猶不欲歸。心凝形釋，與萬化冥合。然後知吾嚮之未始游，游於是乎始，故為之文以志。是歲，元和四年也。（762）

XVI. Little Rock Wall 小石城記

Going north from where the path to West Mountain begins, I crossed Huangmao Ridge. When I came down, there were two paths: one led west, and I followed it but didn't find anything of interest; the other led slightly north then east, and after not more than 400 feet, the dirt trail stopped at a stream, and along the shore was a pile of rocks. The top was shaped like a crenelated beam, and the sides formed walls with what looked like a doorway. I peered inside, but it was pitch-black, so I threw in a small rock and heard a distant splash. It echoed for quite a while before it died away. I circled around and was able to reach the top and could see quite far. Although there wasn't any soil, there were some beautiful trees and a variety of bamboo that was unusually strong. Whether they stood alone or together or leaned down or arched up, the trees and bamboo looked like they had been arranged there by some kind of intelligence.

Indeed, I had long wondered whether or not there was a creator. After coming here, I think there really must be one. And yet I find it odd that they didn't create this in the Central Plains but here in the hinterlands where for hundreds and thousands of years it has had no way to show off its attractions. What a waste of effort! If this god could make such a mistake, maybe they don't really exist. Meanwhile, some say, "This place was created for consoling those worthies who are banished here." And others say, "The spiritual energy here doesn't produce great men, only things like this. Hence, here in southern Ch'u there are few talented men but lots of fine rocks." I don't believe either of these views is correct.

自西山道口徑北，踰黃茅嶺而下，有二道，其一西出，尋之無所得，其一少北而東，不過四十丈，土斷而川分，有積石橫當其垠。其上為睥睨梁欐之形，其旁出堡塢，有若門焉。窺之正黑，投以小石，洞然有水聲，其響之激越，良久乃已。環之可上，望甚遠，無土壤而生嘉樹美箭，益奇而堅，其疏數偃仰，類智者所施設也。

噫，吾疑造物者之有無久矣。及是，愈以為誠有。又怪其不為之於中州，而列是夷狄，更千百年不得一售其伎。是固勞而無用。神者儻不宜如是，則其果無乎。或曰以慰夫賢而辱於此者。或曰其氣之靈不為偉人，而獨為是物，故楚之南少人而多石。是二者，余未信之。 (772)

72-74. FARM LIFE: THREE POEMS 田家三首

ONE

A simple meal and they're off to do chores
before roosters crow and village lanes turn light
they drive their oxen to the edge of their land
and come home from their fields in the dark
accompanied by the scraping of plows
and the flapping of kite wings
they exhaust themselves doing manual work
and they do it all year long
they pay their taxes and perform corvée
meanwhile they go to bed hungry
their children and grandchildren grow older
every generation it's the same

蓐食徇所務，驅牛向東阡。雞鳴村巷白，夜色歸暮田。
札札耒耜聲，飛飛來烏鳶。竭茲筋力事，持用窮歲年。
盡輸助徭役，聊就空自眠。子孫日已長，世世還復然。

TWO

Sitting around fires behind fences
neighbors gather for farm talk at dusk
beyond their yards fall insects are singing
the fields of hemp have finally been cleared
the silk all went to pay taxes
looms lean silent against walls
government lackeys still come by at night
expecting dinners of millet and chicken
they say their boss is high and mighty
they quote his various warnings
"In the county to the east they're late with rent
they claim their carts are stuck in the mud"
officials are seldom forgiving

they beat and flog without mercy
while those who sweat for a living
whose faces are landscapes of misery
seeing the new year already approaching
worry their heels might precede their toes

籬落隔煙火，農談四鄰夕。庭際秋蟲鳴，疏麻方寂歷。
蠶絲盡輸稅，機杼空倚壁。里胥夜經過，雞黍事筵席。
各言官長峻，文字多督責。東鄉後租期，車轂陷泥澤。
公門少推恕，鞭扑恣狼籍。努力慎經營，肌膚真可惜。
迎新在此歲，唯恐踵前跡。

THREE

On a vine-entangled ancient road
beside a winding old wall
the embankments were covered by knotweed
ponds looked clearer in the cold
the harvest was finally over
herders and woodsmen were home before dark
the wind had stripped the willows of leaves
a heavy frost covered the dates
wandering along I lost my way
birds were fighting over places to roost
an old farmer laughed and warned me
"Be careful in the woods after sunset
I harvested a bit extra this year
if you don't mind porridge or gruel"

古道饒蒺藜，縈迴古城曲。蓼花被堤岸，陂水寒更淥。
是時收穫竟，落日多樵牧。風高榆柳疏，霜重梨棗熟。
行人迷去住，野鳥競棲宿。田翁笑相念，昏黑慎原陸。
今年幸少豐，無厭饘與粥。

....
NOTE: Written in Yungchou in the fall of 812.

Two: The last line means to be dragged out of one's home heels first—either dead or off to be flogged.

THREE: Liu was following the old post road that ran along the west shore of the Hsiao not far from his home on the Yuhsi. In the fourth line, some texts give the variant *lu* 綠 (green) in place of *lu* 淥 (clear). (1238)

XVII. THE SNAKE CATCHER 捕蛇者說

The countryside around Yungchou is home to a most unusual snake with a black body and white markings. Any plant it touches dies, and no one it bites survives. But its dried flesh can cure leprosy, paralysis, tumors, and sores and get rid of gangrene and parasites. Hence, it was decreed that anyone who sent two to the royal physician every year would be exempt from public work projects and taxes, and the people of Yungchou vied with each other to catch these snakes.

There was a man surnamed Chiang whose family had specialized in this work for three generations. When I asked Mister Chiang about this, he said, "My grandfather died from snakebite, and my father too. For the past twelve years, I've followed the family trade, and I've nearly died several times too." As he said this, he looked forlorn. Feeling sorry for him, I said, "If you hate it so much, I can ask the authorities to change your public work assignment and you can pay taxes. How would that be?"

Mister Chiang looked even more forlorn, and with tears in his eyes he said, "Show me some pity, Sir. Even though such work is miserable, it's not as miserable as having to pay taxes again. If I didn't do this, I would have come to a bad end long ago. For the past sixty years, three generations of my family have survived in this county, while the lives of our neighbors have gotten worse, as their fields have failed to produce enough to keep them from hunger and want, and they've wailed, then run off and collapsed of hunger and thirst on the roadside, or they've endured the wind and rain, and the heat and cold, and cried out and died of starvation. Their corpses have formed piles. Of my grandfather's generation, there's not one person in ten of whom this isn't true, and of my father's generation, not three in ten. In the twelve years I've been doing this, there's not five in ten, and those who haven't died have left. I've only survived by catching snakes. When government lackeys come to our county, they shout and bully us and make such a racket even the dogs and chickens are afraid. Meanwhile, I get up at night and tiptoe to my pots to see if my snakes are still there, then I lie back down with relief. I take care in feeding them and present them at the appointed time. Then I return home to enjoy my fields and garden and live out my years. Twice a year I risk death, but I'm as happy as I dare be—unlike my neighbors, who have to risk death every day. If I should die right now, I will still have outlived most of them. Why should I hate my trade?"

When I heard this, I felt even sorrier for the man. I used to doubt Confucius's statement, "An oppressive government is worse than a tiger." Having met Mister Chiang, I now believe it. Alas, who would have guessed that people's hatred of taxation would be greater than their hatred of snakes? Thus, I have written this down for those who might be concerned about people's welfare.

永州之野產異蛇，黑質而白章，觸草木盡死，以齧人，無御之者。然得而腊之以為餌，可以已大風攣踠瘻癘，去死肌，殺三蟲。其始，太醫以王命聚之，歲賦其二，募有能捕之者，當其租入，永之人爭奔走焉。

有蔣氏者，專其利三世矣。問之，則曰吾祖死於是，吾父死於是，今吾嗣為之十二年，幾死者數矣。言之，貌若甚慼者。余悲之，且曰若毒之乎。余將告于蒞事者，更若役，復若賦，則何如。

蔣氏大慼，汪然出涕曰君將哀而生之乎。則吾斯役之不幸，未若復吾賦不幸之甚也。嚮吾不為斯役，則久已病矣。自吾氏三世居是鄉，積於今六十歲矣，而鄉鄰之生日蹙，殫其地之出，竭其廬之入，號呼而轉徙，飢渴而頓踣，觸風雨，犯寒暑，呼噓毒癘，往往而死者相藉也。曩與吾祖居者，今其室十無一焉，與吾父居者，今其室十無二三焉，與吾居十二年者，今其室十無四五焉，非死則徒爾。而吾以捕蛇獨存。悍吏之來吾鄉，叫囂乎東西，隳突乎南北，譁然而駭者，雖雞狗不得寧焉。吾恂恂而起，視其缶，而吾蛇尚存，則弛然而臥。謹食之，時而獻焉。退而甘食其土之有，以盡吾齒。蓋一歲之犯死者二焉，其餘則熙熙而樂，豈若吾鄉鄰之旦旦有是哉。今雖死乎此，比吾鄉鄰之死則已後矣，又安敢毒耶。

余聞而愈悲。孔子曰苛政猛於虎也。吾嘗疑乎是，今以蔣氏觀之，猶信。嗚呼，孰知賦斂之毒，有甚是蛇者乎。故為之說，以俟夫觀人風者得焉。

(455)

75. Presented to Chief Minister Li and Assistant Censor Yuan in Lingling, Also Sent to Wu Wu-ling 零陵贈李卿元侍御簡吳武陵

A well-ordered world disdains officials
hence our rustication to the Hsiang
with sunlight filling the four quarters
who needs someone to strike a flint
perching on snags with battered wings
we warble our sad songs to each other
clouds from the north bring a frigid wind
the end of autumn and desolate days
gentlemen prefer to acquiesce
lesser men would rather quarrel
seeing how miserable we look every day
and the sorrow of separation increasing
let's empty this jug of wine
and indulge ourselves in song
too bad no musicians are present
to do these poems of ours justice

理世固輕士，棄捐湘之湄。陽光竟四溟，敲石安所施。
鎩羽集枯榦，低昂互鳴悲。朔雲吐風寒，寂歷窮秋時。
君子尚容與，小人守競危。慘悽日相視，離憂坐自滋。
樽酒聊可酌，放歌諒徒為。惜無協律者，窈眇絃吾詩。

....

NOTE: Written in Yungchou (Lingling) in the late fall of 812 and addressed to Liu's fellow exiles there, Li You-ch'ing 李幼清 and Yuan K'e-chi 元克己. Liu uses the titles of the offices they held prior to their exile. The poem is also addressed to Wu Wu-ling, who was exiled to Yungchou in 808, but who was pardoned in the summer of 812 and had since returned to the capital. (1136)

76. Invited to Accompany Magistrate Wei to the Huang River to Pray for Rain: An Impromptu Poem upon Reaching the Shrine 韋使君黃溪祈雨見召從行至祠下口號

The summer sun exceeded what farmers could bear
our noble lord was worried about the crops
we rode beneath a crescent moon with his aides
their whistles echoed across a sapphire sky
we followed a woodcutter's path to its end
we finally stopped near a rustic dwelling
by a pure cold stream at the mouth of a valley
among ancient trees at a forest shrine
in a damp autumn fog we lit incense
in the first rays of dawn we offered wine
the buzzing flies of a shaman's drone
ritual objects perfectly arranged
an auspicious breeze bent the grass
surely a welcome rain will follow
a sham official waiting to be punished
I offer these words utterly embarrassed

驕陽愆歲事，良牧念蓄畬。列騎低殘月，鳴笛度碧虛。
稍窮樵客路，遙駐野人居。谷口寒流淨，叢祠古木疏。
焚香秋霧濕，奠玉曉光初。肸蠁巫言報，精誠禮物餘。
惠風仍偃草，靈雨會隨車。俟罪非真吏，翻慚奉簡書。

....

NOTE: Written in Yungchou in the fifth month of 813. The magistrate of Yung-chou at this time was Wei Piao 韋彪. Liu was the town's deputy magistrate. It was a post without duties, and he finds himself embarrassed to take part in an official ceremony. High-pitched whistles made from reeds were used to clear a path or to announce the approach of an official. The source of the Huang River is 35 kilometers east of Yungchou (Lingling) as the crow flies. The temple where ceremonies were conducted is gone, but the site is still there in the village of Miaomenkou 廟門口 (Temple Gate). Liu also describes the scenic highlights in one of his travel journals—prose piece XVIII, which follows. (1215)

XVIII. Huang River Excursion 游黃溪記

Among the hundreds of famous mountains and rivers in the counties between Chin to the north, Pin to the west, Wu to the east, and the borders of Ch'u and Yueh here in the south, those of Yungchou are unsurpassed. The administrative area of Yungchou stretches a hundred *li:* north to the Wu River, west to the source of the Hsiang, south to the springs of the Shuang, and east to the Huang River and Tungtun Village. Of the hundreds of villages among these mountains and rivers, those along the Huang are unrivaled.

The Huang is 70 *li* from the city. Walking six hundred paces south from the village of Tungtun, I came to the shrine belonging to the god of the Huang. Above the shrine stood two mountains whose slopes were covered with flowers and foliage, except where there were cliffs and caves. The river was full of small rocks. Wading eighty paces beyond the shrine, I came to the first pool. It was so wonderfully beautiful, it's hard to describe. Basically, it resembled a giant broken pot with thousand-foot sides. As the river's water collected, it looked like a pool of black mascara and moved like moon glow without making a sound, and hundreds of fish rose to the surface and gathered below the boulders. Walking south another hundred paces, I came to the second pool. The boulders there were stupendous and leaned above the current like a mandible of teeth. Below the pool were a group of flat rocks, perfect for a picnic. I saw a bird the size of a crane. It had a red head and black wings and was standing there facing east. As I continued south several more *li,* the landscape didn't change, except the trees were larger and the rocks smaller, and the water made a tinkling sound. As I continued south another *li,* I came to a great plain, where the hills were lower, and the current was slower, and there were fields. When the god of the Huang was human, this was where he lived.

It's said that the river's god was surnamed Wang and that he was related to Wang Mang. When Wang Mang died, the god changed his surname to Huang, and while he was fleeing, he chose this place for its remoteness and hid out here. Wang Mang once said he was a descendant of emperors Huang and Shun. Hence, he named his daughter Princess Huang-huang Shih-chu. Because the sounds for Huang and Wang were similar and also because of the kind of person he was, people thought the story the river god told them sounded likely. Once he settled here, the people lived in peace. Thinking he possessed the Way, after he died, they conducted sacrifices and built a shrine for him. Later, they moved it closer to where they lived, and it's now next to the river on the shady side of the mountain. On the sixteenth day of the fifth month of the year 813, after returning from my visit, I wrote this for those in the future who enjoy excursions.

北之晉，西適豳，東極吳，南至楚越之交，其間名山水而州者以百數，永最善。環永之治百里，北至于浯溪，西至于湘之源，南至于瀧泉，東至于黃溪東屯，其間名山水而村者以百數，黃溪最善。

　黃溪距州治七十里。由東屯南行六百步，至黃神祠。祠之上，兩山牆立，丹碧之華葉駢植，與山升降，其缺者為崖峭巖窟。水之中，皆小石平布。黃神之上，揭水八十步，至初潭。最奇麗，殆不可狀。其略若剖大甕，側立千尺，溪水積焉。黛蓄膏渟，來若白虹，沉沉無聲，有魚數百尾，方來會石下。南去又行百步，至第二潭。石皆巍然，臨浚流，若頷頜齗齶。其下大石雜列，可坐飲食。有鳥赤首烏翼，大如鵠，方東嚮立。自是又南數里，地皆一狀，樹益壯，石益瘦，水鳴皆鏘然。又南一里，至大冥之川，山舒水緩，有土田。始黃神為人時，居其地。

　傳者曰黃神王姓，莽之世也。莽既死，神更號黃氏，逃來，擇其深峭者潛焉。始莽嘗曰余黃虞之後也。故號其女曰黃皇室主。黃與王聲相邇，而又有本，其所以傳言者益驗。神既居是，民咸安焉。以為有道，死乃俎豆之，為立祠。後稍徙近乎民，今祠在山陰溪水上。元和八年五月十六日，既歸為記，以啟後之好游者。

....

NOTE: Liu Tsung-yuan's ability to travel outside the town of Yungchou and its immediate vicinity was restricted and required advance notice as well as someone to oversee such excursions. This overnight visit to the Huang River was, as far as I know, the only time he was allowed to travel that far during his ten-year exile. The first sentence marks the limits of Chinese territory during the second millennium BC: the state of Chin controlled what is now Shansi province; Pin controlled Kansu province; Wu controlled Kiangsu province; Ch'u controlled Hupei, Hunan, and Kiangsi provinces; and Yueh controlled Chekiang province. The Wu River is a tributary of the Hsiang, and the Shuang is a branch of the North River in Kuangtung province. Wang Mang staged a coup in the first century AD that brought an end to the Han dynasty and his own short-lived dynasty. Emperor Huang, or Huang-ti (the Yellow Emperor), established the hegemony of the Chinese in China's Central Plains. Both he and Emperor Shun lived in the middle of the third millennium BC. (759)

77. Hearing a Gibbon on the Huang River
入黃溪聞猿

The riverside path winds for miles
where is that gibbon howling
this banished official has no more tears
its heartbreaking cries are in vain

溪路千里曲，哀猿何處鳴。孤臣淚已盡，虛作斷腸聲。

....

NOTE: Written in Yungchou in the fifth month of 813. The Huang River is a major tributary of the Hsiang, into which it empties near the modern city of Yungchou to the north, not ancient Yungchou (Lingling). There are no longer any gibbons along the Huang, but sections of the river are currently protected for their natural beauty. The terms of Liu's exile did not normally allow him to go so far afield, but since he was asked to accompany the magistrate, this was a rare opportunity for him to indulge his love of exploration. (1215)

78. Written at the First Sign of White Hair about the Pomegranate I Planted 始見白髮題所植海石榴樹

It's been a few years since I planted this sweet thing
my cheeks aren't the same as its blooms anymore
henceforth I won't speak of spring anymore
looking at this old bush then this old man

幾年封植愛芳叢，韶艷朱顏竟不同。從此休論上春事，看成古木對衰翁。

....

Note: Written in Yungchou in 813, three years after planting the pomegranate mentioned in poem 55. (1230)

79. At Scholar Tuan Chiu's Place Reading Lines in a Letter from Our Deceased Friend, Lu of Hengchou 段九秀才處見亡友呂衡州書跡

My friendship with Lu was the dearest of my life
when he served in Hengyang his body multiplied
suddenly from your sleeve some lines of his appeared
seeing my old friend I had to wipe the tears

交呂平生意最親，衡陽往事似分身。袖中忽見三行字，拭淚相看是故人。

....

NOTE: Written in Yungchou most likely in early 814. Lu Wen served as magistrate of Hengchou (aka Hengyang), hence the name given him here. He was Liu Tsung-yuan's older cousin and a lifelong confidant. He died in autumn of 811 shortly after arriving at his post. Tuan Chiu, or Tuan Hung-ku 段弘古, visited Liu in Yungchou on several occasions, the last time being the spring of 814. He was friends with both men and died in autumn of 814. In the first line, I've used the variant 呂 (the surname Lu) in place of 侶 (companion). The second line refers to Lu's attention to his duties rather than the power to manifest multiple bodies. (1184)

80. HEARING AN ORIOLE 聞黃鸝

I was tired of hearing cuckoos day and night
suddenly I realized an oriole was singing
interrupting my Ch'u River dream
I could see my old garden and it was spring
no mountains or rivers as far as I could see
a horizon instead of green waves of grain
taxes and corvée are light in the royal realm
farmers make wine and have time to socialize
this time of year when the sky finally clears
they yell back and forth down every village lane
above Kunming Lake soaring in the sunshine
birds can't help notice the new catkins
and here I am among a million mountains
feeling like a refugee with no hope of returning
why has this bird come from my home
reminding me of my catalpa and mulberry trees
stop singing and fly back as fast as you can
the mulberries in the west garden should be ripe when you arrive

倦聞子規朝暮聲，不意忽有黃鸝鳴。一聲夢斷楚江曲，滿眼故園春意生。
目極千里無山河，麥芒際天搖青波。王畿優本少賦役，務閑酒熟饒經過。
此時晴煙最深處，舍南巷北遙相語。翻日迴度崑明飛，凌風邪看細柳鬌。
我今誤落千萬山，身同儃人不思還。鄉禽何事亦來此，令我生心憶桑梓。
閉聲迴翅歸務速，西林紫椹行當熟。

....

NOTE: Written in Yungchou in the spring of 814. Cuckoos usually start
calling in the second lunar month and don't stop until the fourth month.
The Ch'u River here refers to the Hsiang and to the way home. Southwest of
Ch'ang-an, Kunming Lake was a favorite destination for those at court with
spare time. Mulberries were grown for their leaves, which were used to feed
silkworms. Catalpas were grown for their lumber but also for the wax from
their seedpods, which was used to make candles. (1249)

81. White Poplar Flower 楊白花

White poplar flower
blown across the Yangtze
depriving the royal garden of its beauty
spreads the glow of spring a million miles away
as the first rays of dawn light Eternal Autumn Palace
from the ceaseless lament the crows take flight

楊白花，風吹渡江水。坐令宮樹無顏色，搖蕩春光千萬里。
茫茫曉日下長秋，哀歌未斷城鴉起。

....

NOTE: Written in Yungchou in the spring of 814. The poplar flower (the fuzz
or gossamer that unravels from the catkins in spring) here refers to the lover
of Empress Hu of the Northern Wei dynasty. His name was Yang Hua 楊花
(Poplar Flower). Worried that his relationship with the empress would lead
to his undoing, he fled south across the Yangtze to the state of Liang and
never returned. Heartbroken, the empress composed the song "White Poplar
Flower." Liu uses the title and theme for his own lament. In the penultimate
line, he refers to the palace in Loyang where the empress lived. (1251)

82. Sent in Thanks on a Moonlit Night in Early Autumn to Scholar Lou Recuperating from Illness at Kaiyuan Temple
酬婁秀才寓居開元寺早秋月夜病中見寄

A traveler thinks of his garden back home
on the Hsiaohsiang River it's his nightly malaise
recuperating in a layman's room
he circles the hills of the feathered race in his dreams
having tasted the Tao he is easily content
forsaking fame he seeks within himself
his bare walls lit by a waning moon
inside his door insects anticipate fall
the pair of golden cups you sent by mistake
are hard to repay with this inferior jade
there aren't any shortcuts to the highest heavens
and this likely won't help free you from cares

客有故園思，瀟湘生夜愁。病依居士室，夢繞羽人丘。
味道憐知止，遺名得自求。壁空殘月曙，門掩候蟲秋。
謬委雙金重，難徵雜珮酬。碧宵無枉路，徒此助離憂。

. . . .

NOTE: Written in Yungchou in the fall of 814. Lou T'u-nan followed Liu to Yungchou in 806 and lived there for several years. In 808 he left briefly for Kueichou and again in 810 for the Huainan region, for which see poem 60. Lou returned from that trip in 812. Shortly afterward, he became ill and moved into Kaiyuan Temple 開元寺, a Buddhist monastery less than a kilometer outside Yungchou's South Gate. Here it is two years later, and he's still there. Monasteries often provided accommodations for the educated class regardless of their spiritual affiliation. Lou was a student of Taoism, and among the places Taoist adepts hoped to visit were the Cinnabar Hills, which could only be reached through the air. Among the goals of such practice was ascension to the Nine Heavens. Beyond Yungchou, the combined waters of the Hsiao and the Hsiang were usually referred to as the Hsiang. But the combination of their names, as here and elsewhere in Liu's poems, was also common. The

Chinese say crickets move indoors at the first sign of autumn. The "golden cups" and "inferior jade" are polite terms for the exchange of poems between Lou and Liu. Thus, the word "this" in the tenth and twelfth lines refers to the poem Liu is sending his recuperating friend. (1133)

XIX. Lunghsing Temple's East Hill 永州龍興寺東丘記

Views worthy of an excursion are chiefly of two sorts: the expansive and the restricted, these and no others. Where a trail rises above a mountain pass, or penetrates a jungle and opens up to grand vistas, this is the expansive sort. And where one encounters hills and mounds that offer a view of vegetation pressing in and of being surrounded, this is the restricted sort. In cases of the expansive type, even were one to add lofty terraces or rambling pavilions for following the course of the sun and stars or for looking out upon the wind and rain, one wouldn't complain about them getting in the way. In cases of the restricted sort, even were one to add dense groves and masses of rocks to create caves and valleys, one wouldn't complain about such things closing it off.

What I've called East Hill is of the restricted sort. It was abandoned land outside the temple when I acquired and enclosed it, which I did by connecting it to the temple's northern boundary. Where there were hollows and scarps, I didn't get rid of their original form. But I screened them off with dense bamboo and connected it all with a winding bridge. I also added over three hundred trees: cassias, locusts, pines, firs, and mahogany, as well as ornamental plants and unusual-looking rocks, and laid everything out in a grid, with all the green foliage providing shade and privacy. Those who visit walk this way and that without seeing how to get out. The air is pleasant and never hot, and cool breezes arise by themselves. A small pavilion and a tiny hut round out the sense of seclusion. And yet, those who have been there have sometimes complained that it's too confining.

Truly, Lunghsing is a jewel among the temples of Yungchou. Climbing to the top of its highest hall, one can see the horizon to the south. And opening its main gate, one can see the Hsiang—such are its expansive views. As for this small hill, if someone were to clear it and lay it bare, this would be to reduce what I have called the two kinds of views by one and would destroy what is appropriate to the place. The seclusion of this hill provides a place to relax. Its solitude provides a place to reflect. The humidity of summer disappears the moment you reach its base. And a sense of peace that can't be driven off is waiting at its summit. Who will join me in losing themselves on this hill? Not possessing the virtue of Duke

Shao, and fearing that it all might be destroyed, I'm writing this for those noble souls of the future.

游之適，大率有二，曠如也，奧如也，如斯而已。其地之凌阻峭，出幽鬱，寥廓悠長，則於曠宜，抵丘垤，伏灌莽，迫邃迴合，則於奧宜。因其曠，雖增以崇臺延閣，迴環日星，臨瞰風雨，不可病其敵也。因其奧，雖增以茂樹聚石，穿若洞谷，蓊若林麓，不可病其邃也。

今所謂東丘者，奧之宜者也。其始龕之外棄地，余得而合焉，以屬於堂之北陲。凡坳洼坻岸之狀，無廢其故。屏以密竹，聯以曲梁。桂檜松杉楩柟之植，幾三百本，嘉卉美石，又經緯之。俛入綠縟，幽蔭薈蔚。步武錯迕，不知所出。溫風不爍，清氣自至。小亭陋室，曲有奧趣。然而至焉者，往往以邃為病。

噫，龍興，永之佳寺也。登高殿可以望南極，闢大門可以瞰湘流，若是其曠也。而於是小丘，又將披而攘之，則吾所謂游有二者，無乃闕焉而喪其地之宜乎。丘之幽幽，可以處休。丘之窅窅，可以觀妙。溽暑遁去，茲丘之下。大和不遷，茲丘之巔。奧乎茲丘，孰從我游。余無召公之德，懼蔽伐之及也，故書以祈後之君子。

....

NOTE: Liu wrote this in Yungchou on the fifth day of the first month of 815, just before leaving to return to Ch'ang-an. Apparently he wanted to make sure this landscape he created near his former monastic residence would not be leveled, or if it were, that a record of it survived. Duke Shao was an ancient paragon of virtue of the first millenium BC. (748)

83. Presented in Reply to Supernumerary Tou Ch'ang of Langchou, Who Sent Liu Twenty-Eight a Poem and Urged Me to Write Back and to Hurry There 朗州竇常員外寄劉二十八詩見促行騎走筆酬贈

I've been stuck in this backwater close to twelve years
recently a summons reached my poor door
I imagined myself in Chuang-tzu's dream
I felt like Su Wu going home
the jade bracelet I received is still ringing
your team of horses is urging mine on
I don't envy the geese in Hengyang anymore
we're all flying north this spring

投荒垂一紀，新詔下荊扉。疑比莊周夢，情如蘇武歸。
賜環留逸響，五馬助征騑。不羨衡陽雁，春來前後飛。

....

NOTE: Written in Yungchou in the first half of the first month of 815 upon being recalled to Ch'ang-an. Tou Ch'ang was serving as magistrate of Langchou—an old name for Changte, 300 kilometers north of Yungchou and just west of where the Hsiang flows into Tungting Lake. Liu addresses him by the title he held previously at the Water Bureau. Liu Yu-hsi was the same town's assistant magistrate and was sometimes addressed as the twenty-eighth male born in his generation in his clan. He was also recalled and was waiting for Liu Tsung-yuan to join him. One measurement of time in China was the twelve-year period it took Jupiter to complete its path around the sun. Liu is rounding up here, as his exile lasted just under ten years. In his famous self-titled book, Chuang-tzu once dreamed he was a butterfly. When he woke up, he wondered if he wasn't a butterfly dreaming he was Chuang-tzu. Su Wu was an imperial envoy during the Han dynasty who was captured by the Huns and spent nineteen years in captivity before he was released. The emperor gave those he recalled, or expected to recall, a gift of a jade bracelet. As a magistrate, Tou Ch'ang was authorized to use a team of five horses for official purposes and is urging Liu to stop dallying. Hengyang, the next major city downstream, was as far south as geese migrated, or so people said. Liu left Yungchou by boat, not by horse. (1150)

84. Recalled to the Capital, I Send This to Friends Back in Lingling 詔追赴都迴寄零陵親故

I keep thinking about this minnow in that tiny pond
then I worry about these puny wings trying to reach Heaven
I've lost count of the markers along the shore
each one farther from where we parted

每憶纖鱗遊尺澤，翻愁弱羽上丹霄。岸傍古堠應無數，次弟行看別路遙。

....

NOTE: Written in the middle of the first month of 815 on the way back to Ch'ang-an. Lingling was an old name for Yungchou. Liu thinks about the decade he spent there and his impending return to the empyrean heights at court. Major roads and waterways in China were lined with distance markers every 5 *li* (2.5 kilometers). (1148)

85. THE WATERFALL AT CHIEHWEI CLIFF 界圍巖水簾

Where Chiehwei Cliff welcomes the Hsiang
where its green walls embrace the transparent water
a suspended stream forms a glittering curtain
unreeling silk that never ends
beating on stones of the darkest jade
the percussion penetrates every rocky recess
crowning the ridge sunset-colored clouds
resemble something from a celestial journey
it's hard to describe such a magical scene
such an unexpected work of the gods
it reminds me of the emperor at court
the gems hanging from his royal hat
when the minister of Ch'u was banished to the South
he hoped to reach the Cinnabar Hills
I'm finally heading back north
I've been recalled and freed from my shackles
seeking transcendence is what I'd prefer
but serving the country won't wait
I'll have to return in my eremitic dreams
having lingered too long I urged the boatman on

界圍匯湘曲，青壁環澄流。懸泉粲成簾，羅注無時休。
韻磬叩凝碧，鏘鏘徹巖幽。丹霞冠其巔，想像凌虛游。
靈境不可狀，鬼工諒難求。忽如朝玉皇，天冕垂前旒。
楚臣昔南逐，有意仍丹丘。我今始北旋，新詔釋縲囚。
采真誠眷戀，許國無淹留。再來寄幽夢，遺貯催行舟。

....

NOTE: Written in the middle of the first month of 815 on the way back to
Ch'ang-an. After nearly ten years in exile, Liu was recalled and is traveling
by boat down the Hsiang toward the Yangtze. The location of this cliff and its
waterfall is unknown. It doesn't appear in any of Liu's accounts of the area.
Most commentators are of the opinion it was somewhere between Yungchou
and Hengchou (Hengyang). The name means "border wall," which presum-

ably refers to the border between the two administrative regions. In ancient times, emperors wore flat-topped hats with strands of jewels hanging in front. The minister of the ancient state of Ch'u referred to here was the poet Ch'u Yuan (340–278 BC), who was also banished to the Hsiang for his unwelcome advice. The Cinnabar Hills were the home of Taoist immortals. Liu didn't have to wait for a dream to return. He passed this cliff again two months later. (1137)

86. Passing Hengshan and Seeing Buds Opening, I Send This to My Cousin 過衡山見新花開却寄弟

We've been away from the gardens of the capital too long
the southfacing branches are blooming here in Ch'u
clear skies and the road home are waiting to lead you back
it's the time of year when geese turn north at the peak

故國名園久別離，今朝楚樹發南枝。晴天歸路好相逐，正是峰前迴雁時。

....

NOTE: Written in the middle of the first month of 815 near Hengyang on the way back to Ch'ang-an. Liu's cousin Liu Tsung-chih was ill and still in Yung-chou. Thinking he would recover, Liu tries to encourage him to follow him back to the capital. But his cousin didn't recover and died later that year at the age of thirty-three. The sacred mountain of Hengshan, whose seventy-two peaks stretch from Hengyang all the way north to Changsha, was said to be as far south as geese migrated. Yungchou, Hengyang, and Changsha were the major cities in the southernmost part of the ancient state of Ch'u. (1148)

87. ENCOUNTERING WIND ON THE MILO 汨羅遇風

I experienced the South but not the Ch'u minister's grief
I'll be entering the royal gates again full of hope
on my way past the Milo I told the spring wind
don't let the waves ruin this auspicious time

南來不作楚臣悲，重入脩門自有期。為報春風汨羅道，莫將波浪枉明時。

....

NOTE: Written in the second half of the first month of 815 on the way back to
the capital. Liu was traveling by boat down the Hsiang toward the Yangtze.
Just north of where the Hsiang merges with the waters of Tungting Lake, so
does the Milo. The Ch'u minister here refers to Ch'u Yuan, who drowned
himself in the Milo when he heard Ch'u had been conquered by the state of
Ch'in. The gates refer to those of the palace in Ch'ang-an. (1149)

88. Having Failed to Get Drunk on Departure Wine, I Send This Back from a Post Station to Those Who Saw Me Off 離觴不醉至驛却寄相送諸公

You all said goodbye to the only sober person there
I arrived at this rest stop miserable and lonely
no companions from Kaoyang met me in Chingchou
all night a spring chill filled inn

無限居人送獨醒，可憐寂寞到長亭。荊州不遇高陽侶，一夜春寒滿下廳。

....

NOTE: Written near the end of the first month of 815 on the way back to Ch'ang-an—a week to ten days after leaving Yungchou. Liu is stopping for the night at an inn on the north shore of the Yangtze near Chingchou (modern Chiangling), which was the seat of government for all the districts to the south, including Yungchou. Kaoyang was the name of a lake outside Chingchou known for outings and banquets. It was also known as the place where Liu Pang 劉邦 met Chih Shih-ch'i 酈食其, the Crazy Man of Kaoyang 高陽狂生. Chih was known for his forthrightness and became an important adviser to Liu Pang in his quest to restore the Han dynasty. Liu Tsung-yuan wishes he had someone like Chih to help him navigate his return to court politics. To ensure the rapid transmission of documents and mail, the government established rest stops every 2.5 kilometers on major roads and inns every 5. (1151)

89. On My Way Back to the Capital I Climbed the Plateau North of Hanyang and Wrote This at the Linchuan Post Station 北還登漢陽北原題臨川驛

As I hurried toward palace gates
I stopped to look around Linchuan
I wasn't embarrassed by the rubble
I was saddened nothing had been done
a few pines marked where there used to be a temple
traces of snow where there once were terraced fields
the scenes of village life were depressing
after so many years the place still looks hopeless

驅車方向闕，迴首一臨川。多壘非余耻，無謀終自憐。
亂松知野寺，餘雪記山田。惆悵樵漁事，今還又落然。

....

NOTE: Written at the end of the first month of 815. After reaching Chingchou, instead of continuing north, Liu traveled east to where the Han River merges with the Yangtze. Where it does, the town of Hanyang is on the Han's west shore and Hankou on its east shore. Liu stayed here with his father in 783 when he was twelve. In 781, imperial armies put down a rebellion in this region, and Liu returns to see the place still hasn't recovered. Although he doesn't feel responsible for the devastation, he regrets having not been able to help with the recovery and indirectly criticizes the court's policies regarding disaffected areas. (1152)

90. AT SHANHSUEH POST STATION WITH LIU MENG-TE OFFERING A LIBATION FOR MISTER CH'UN YU

善謔驛和劉夢得酹淳于先生

The swan flew off at the river
but a bird still sang at court
Ch'un Yu's excuse was praised in Ch'u
his fame was certain when he rescued Ch'i
a thousand years later at his weed-covered grave
it's hard to lift my cup twice
Liu Ling today must be thinking
the times are different but the story is the same

水上鵠已去，庭中鳥又鳴。辭因使楚重，名為救齊成。
荒壟遽千古，羽觴難再傾。劉伶今日意，異代是同聲。

....

NOTE: Written at the beginning of the second month of 815 near Hsiangyang 襄陽, a few days after the previous poem. Liu Meng-te was Liu Yu-hsi's sobriquet. He too had been recalled. I'm not sure why the two men didn't meet in Langchou, where Liu Yu-hsi had been serving, or failing that in Chingchou, on the north shore of the Yangtze. If they did, neither Liu Yu-hsi nor Liu Tsung-yuan mentions it. Perhaps Liu Tsung-yuan reached Chingchou ahead of his friend and decided to take a side trip to Hanyang while waiting for him to catch up. In any case, from this point on they traveled back to Ch'ang-an together. The Shanhsueh post station was 50 kilometers southeast of Hsiangyang near the grave of Ch'un Yu 淳于 (ca. 386–310 BC), or Ch'un Yu-k'un 淳于髡. Ch'un was a minister in the ancient state of Ch'i and was ordered to take a swan to present to the king of Ch'u. Ch'un released the bird instead shortly after leaving the Ch'i capital and proceeded to Ch'u with an empty cage. When he arrived, he told the king of Ch'u that when he stopped at the river near the Shanhsueh post station, he thought the bird was thirsty and let it out of its cage to drink, and the bird flew off. The king admired Ch'un for his honesty (sic). On another occasion Ch'un likened himself to a bird at court, and the king urged him to sing, which he did much to the consternation of others at court. On yet another occasion he cajoled the king of Ch'i into sending more presents than he had planned to the king of Chao but thereby gained Chao's help in fending off a threatened invasion by Ch'u. Liu Ling (221–300) was one of the Seven Sages of the Bamboo Grove. To avoid the shifting political allegiances at court, he stayed drunk. Liu Tsung-yuan uses him here as a stand-in for his friend Liu Yu-hsi, who also wrote a poem on this occasion. Liu Yu-hsi's poem ends: "I brought a barrel of wine / to place before your graveside trees" 我有一石酒, 置君墳樹前. Liu Tsung-yuan is clearly not an admirer of Ch'un Yu, finding it difficult to offer anything more than the formal first cup of wine, while his friend offers Ch'un a whole barrel. In the second line, I've opted for the variant *t'ing* 庭 (court) in place of *t'ing* 亭 (pavilion), as it conforms better with the backstory. (1153)

91. Regarding the Bamboo at the Chingshui Post Station, Where Mister Chao of Tienshui Says He Planted Twelve of the Canes Himself
清水驛叢竹天水趙云余手種一十二莖

Twelve canes of bamboo below the eaves
convey the deep feelings of a Hsiangyang official
Ling Lun should come see these himself
and write about the pairs of phoenix-like calls

簷下疏篁十二莖，襄陽從事寄幽情。祇應更使伶倫見，寫盡雌雄雙鳳鳴。

....

NOTE: Written at the beginning of the second month of 815 a day or so after the previous poem. The Chingshui post station was just south of Hsiangyang. A local official there surnamed Chao presented the two men with twelve lengths of bamboo. According to a story in the *History of the Han Dynasty* 漢書/律歷志, the Yellow Emperor once sent Ling Lun to gather bamboo in a certain valley. He brought back twelve lengths and made them into panpipes that sounded like six male and six female phoenixes. (1163)

92. Li Hsi-ch'uan's Zither Sounding Stone
李西川薦琴石

Long ago Chou Chi played a zither that could sing
he played the southern style favored by Emperor Shun
stones from other mountains shall forever sound dull
a far subtler music comes from generosity

遠師騶忌鼓鳴琴，去和南風愜舜心。從此他山千古重，殷勤曾是奉徽音。

....

NOTE: Written at the beginning of the second month of 815 a day or so after
the previous poem. After following the Han River upstream from Hanyang's
Linchuan post station and past the Shanhsueh post station to Hsiangyang,
Liu Tsung-yuan and Liu Yu-hsi then switched to overland travel. Li Hsi-
ch'uan (757–823), or Li Yi-chien 李夷簡, was a distant relative of the founder
of the T'ang dynasty and was serving as magistrate of Hsiangyang. Li's previ-
ous post was that of military commissioner of Hsichuan (Western Szechuan)
and is the name by which he is referred to here. Chou Chi (385–319 BC) was
an ancient zither master. He was also an adviser to the king of Ch'i and often
couched his advice in terms of the harmonies he played. Emperor Shun (r
2233–2383 BC) was one of Liu's heroes and was known for developing the
"southern style" for zither players. To improve the resonance of their instru-
ments, musicians often placed their zithers on top of a table or a stone slab.
The last line suggests Li presented Liu with this particular stone. (1154)

93–94. Reply to Senior Attendant Gentleman Yang in Thanks for Sending His Eighth Uncle Shih-yi to Present This Jest to Guests Summoned Back from the South: Two Poems
奉酬楊侍郎丈因送八叔拾遺戲贈詔追南來渚賓二首

One

The pine tree note brought by Chen-yi
calmed these returning geese wary of bowstrings
who is in charge now in Hanlin's hushed halls
that phoenix songbird should be flying to Heaven soon

貞一來時松彩牋，一行歸鴈慰驚弦。翰林寂寞誰為主，鳴鳳應須早上天。

Two

After serving our sentences we're finally returning
our southern exile they've announced is over
but Yeh Ch'ang was freed from his shackles
Eastern Chou times are long gone

一生判却歸休，謂著南冠到頭。冶長雖解縲絏，無由得見東周。

....

NOTE: Written in the middle of the second month of 815 just before reaching Ch'ang-an.

ONE: Chen-yi was the sobriquet of Yang Shih-yi. He was the uncle of Liu's friend Yang Yu-ling 楊於陵 (753–830) and the eighth-born male in his generation of his clan. Chen-yi's daughter was married to Liu Yu-hsi's eldest son, hence he was only too happy to meet the returning exiles on their way to the capital and to convey the note from his nephew. Apparently, the note included a painting of a pine, a symbol of long life and also of welcome—what famous mountain in China doesn't have a Welcoming Pine? The Hanlin Academy was the imperial court's most prestigious body and was in charge of drafting decrees and summons. Calling it "hushed" is meant to emphasize its function as a place where decrees were written, not discussed. The phoenix often refers to the emperor, but here it refers to the impending elevation of Chen-yi to become the director of the Academy.

Two: A rare example of a quatrain using six syllables to the line, rather than five or seven. It was the form favored by the exiled poet Ch'u Yuan. According to the *Analects of Confucius* (5.1): "The Master said, 'Yeh Ch'ang would make a good son-in-law. Even though he is in shackles, he committed no crime.' The Master therefore gave him his daughter in marriage." Confucius lived during the Eastern Chou dynasty (771–221 BC). Liu sees himself marked by his exile (despite having "committed no crime") and not likely to be accepted back at a court devoid of Confucius's more forgiving perspective. (1157)

95. Reaching the Pa River Pavilion in the Second Month after Being Summoned Back to the Capital 詔追赴都二月至灞亭上

Eleven years ago I was a southbound exile
after four thousand *li* I'm in the North again
together with the summons warm weather arrived too
along the postal route new flowers every day

十一年前南渡客，四千里外北歸人。詔書許逐陽和至，驛路開花處處新。

....

NOTE: Written in the second half of the second month of 815 after having followed spring north to Ch'ang-an. The Pa River Pavilion was 10 kilometers east of the capital and was where people often welcomed or said goodbye to friends. According to Liu Yu-hsi, the two men spent the night there before continuing into the city. They arrived from the southeast via the Wukuan Pass. Throughout his month-long journey, Liu felt as if the world itself rejoiced at his return. As elsewhere, he adds a year to the length of his exile—such is the nature of exile. The distance from Yungchou to the capital on the government postal route via the Wukuan Pass was 3,200 *li*, or 1,000 miles, but once Liu reached the Yangtze, instead of continuing north, he made a side trip to Hanyang and added another 800 *li* to his trip. (1154)

96. Along the Road Past Shangshan There Was a Lone Pine to Which Someone Took an Ax for More Light. A Kind Person Took Pity and Built a Bamboo Fence around What Remained, and It Responded with New Growth. Moved, I Wrote This Poem
商山臨路有孤松往來斫以為明好事者憐之編竹成援遂其生植感而賦詩

A lone pine shaded a rest stop with green
putting down roots beside a dirt road
it didn't need to guard against the heights
it was injured for the sake of more light
luckily a kindhearted person came along
surrounding it with a fence
part of its heart survived
enough to feel the rain and dew

孤松停翠蓋，託根臨黃路。不以險自防，遂為明所誤。
幸逢仁惠意，重此藩籬護。猶有半心存，時將承雨露。

....

NOTE: Liu's stay in Ch'ang-an lasted less than a month. This poem was written, or at least experienced, in the second half of the third month of 815, a few days after leaving the capital. The route Liu chose to his new place of exile was across the Chungnan Mountains, again via Wukuan Pass. Shangshan is the name of a mountain northwest of the pass. Liu, of course, identifies with the pine. (1158)

97. On the Hsiang Again 再上湘江

Hello waters of the Hsiang
I'm back on you again today
who knows once I leave you
when I'll return from yet another exile

好在湘江水，今朝又上來。不知從此去，更遣幾時回。

....

NOTE: Written in the middle of the fourth month of 815. After crossing the
waters of the Yangtze and Tungting Lake, Liu continued his journey up the
Hsiang to his new place of exile. He was accompanied by Liu Yu-hsi as far as
Hengyang. (1162)

98. On South Tower in front of the Changsha Post Station Reflecting on the Past 長沙驛前南樓感舊

Ever since that sea crane left
I've heard no news for thirty years
I can't hold the tears back today
standing alone on the station's south tower

海鶴一為別，存亡三十秋。今來數行淚，獨上驛南樓。

. . . .

NOTE: Written in the middle of the fourth month of 815. On his way up the Hsiang River to his new place of exile, Liu stopped at the government post station in Changsha. In an early edition of Liu's poems, this note appears after the title: "I once said goodbye to Mister Te 德公 here." Although nothing more is known about this man, in Liu's day the term "sea crane" referred to someone leaving on a long journey. Thirty years earlier, Liu was thirteen and accompanying his father on a journey through this region. My guess is that Mister Te was on his way into exile and made an impression on the young Liu—hence, the tears, for Mister Te and himself, not to mention for his father. (1164)

99. Presented on Parting from Meng-te in Hengyang 衡陽與夢得分路贈別

Back in the capital after ten weary years
who would have guessed we'd be bound beyond the ridges
on Wave-Queller's old road amid mist and wind
past his busted statue and overgrown shrine
being rash and lazy we earned the scorn of others
how could skill with words ensure our reputations
there's no need to part at the river today
we can wash our hat ties in this waterfall of tears

十年憔顇到秦京，誰料翻為嶺外行。伏波故道風煙在，翁仲遺墟草樹平。
直以慵疏招物議，休將文字占時名。今朝不用臨河別，垂淚千行便濯纓。

....

NOTE: Written in Hengyang near the end of the fourth month of 815. Liu is continuing by boat to Liuchou in Kuanghsi province, while his friend Liu Yu-hsi (Meng-te) is heading overland to Lienchou in Kuantung province. Before they left Ch'ang-an, Liu successfully petitioned the court to let the two men switch posts, as Liu Yu-hsi was traveling with his mother, and Lienchou was a much nearer post. The two provinces of Kuangtung and Kuanghsi were separated from the Yangtze watershed by a set of five ridges both men had yet to cross. General Ma Yuan 馬授 (14 BC–AD 49), known as Wave-Queller, led an army of 20,000 soldiers and a navy of 2,000 ships into this region during the Han dynasty to put down a series of rebellions and to open it up to greater central-government control. He died during this campaign but has long been remembered for his efforts. The shrine built in his honor at the Hsiang River town of Lukou 淥口 still exists but apparently wasn't doing well when Tsung-yuan and Yu-hsi visited just before they reached Hengyang. The last couplet refers to the custom of washing the ties that held one's hat in place when taking up a new post and to the story of two men who washed theirs in a river when saying goodbye. Liu Yu-hsi responded to this poem with the following verse. (1159)

Sent to Lienchou Once More and Arriving in Hengchou I Offer This in Response to the Parting Gift of Liu of Liuchou 再授連州至衡州酬柳柳州贈別 by Liu Yu-hsi

We were banished ten years then recalled
a thousand miles on the Hsiang and our roads fork once more
I'm off to serve again but not like Chancellor Huang
nor like Teacher Liu whose fame grew with every exile
I'll watch migrating geese until they're gone
and my heart will break every time I hear a gibbon
sailing east on the Kuei when you pass Lienshan Mountain
look my way and sing "I'm Thinking of Someone" loud

去國十年同赴召，渡湘千里又分歧。重臨事異黃承相，三黜名漸柳士師。
歸目併隨迴鴈盡，愁腸正遇斷猿時。桂江東過連山下，相望長吟有所思。

....

Note: Liu Yu-hsi was initially exiled to Lienchou in 805, but on his way there, his assignment was changed to Langchou. Hence, this was the second time he was sent to Lienchou. During the Han dynasty, Chancellor Huang Pa 黃霸 was twice sent away from the capital to serve in the countryside, but his reputation only grew each time. Liu-hsia-hui 柳下惠 was thrice forced into retirement but kept coming back to serve, saying, "What else am I going to do?" (*Analects* 18.2). Liu-hsia-hui was, incidentally, Liu Tsung-yuan's ancestor, Chan Huo, who acquired "liu" meaning "willow" for his surname from his practice of sitting under a willow when teaching. Liu Yu-hsi anticipates that once they part, Liu Tsung-yuan will take the Kuei (or Li) River southeast as far as Wuchou 梧州, then head west on the Hsun River to his new place of exile. "I'm Thinking of Someone" was an ancient Han-dynasty song that began, "I'm thinking of someone / in the far South Seas." Yu-hsi asks his friend to sing it loud enough for him to hear as Tsung-yuan passes near his new place of exile. He uses Lien*shan* in place of Lienchou, as Lienshan was a bit closer to where the Kuei meets the Hsun—but still 150 kilometers away. (1160)

100. Parting from Meng-te Again 重別夢德

We've followed the same path for the past twenty years
suddenly this morning we're taking separate roads
if imperial grace should permit us to return
let's spend our last years living next to farmers

二十年來萬事同，今朝岐路忽西東。皇恩若許歸田去，晚歲當為鄰舍翁。

. . . .

NOTE: Written in Hengyang near the end of the fourth month of 815 on Liu's way to his new place of exile. Liu Yu-hsi (Meng-te) and Liu Tsung-yuan knew each other as students, passed the civil service exam the same year (793), and served in several posts together until both were exiled in 805. All they can hope for now is "imperial grace" and a future limited to farming rather than serving at court. Liu couldn't get T'ao Yuan-ming out of his mind. To this, his fellow exile responded with the following poem. (1160)

Replying Again to Liu of Liuchou 重答柳柳州 by Liu Yu-hsi

Already as students we shared old-man worries
parting here today I keep thinking back to this
if we have a chance to retire somewhere together
let's quit these jobs the first sign of white hair

弱冠同懷長者憂，臨歧回想盡悠悠。耦耕若便遺身世，黃髮相看萬事休。

101. Third Poem for Vice Director Liu 三贈劉員外

We deceived ourselves trusting books
our mistake became clear at work
here where our paths part today
what year can I expect you back

信書成自誤，經事漸知非。今日臨歧別，何年待汝歸。

....

NOTE: Written near the end of the fourth month of 815 in Hengyang. Liu
uses Liu Yu-hsi's job title at the time of their exile ten years earlier when
both served as vice directors in the central government: Liu Tsung-yuan in
the Ministry of Rites, and Liu Yu-hsi in the Department of State Affairs. The
earliest dynastic records and predynastic accounts provided the material on
which the view of good government was based in China. Actual practice,
of course, differed, but this is what candidates were examined on and what
officials were criticized for not following. Even today, there are laws in China
promulgated by different ministries that require opposite actions, or non-
actions. Once again, Liu Yu-hsi replied with a poem. These were the third
poems the two exchanged in Hengyang before they parted for the last time.
(1161)

In Reply to Liu Tzu-hou 答柳子厚 by Liu Yu-hsi

We haven't lived as long as Po-yu
yet we've already suffered more than four sorrows
I'm ready to stop this riding around
let's escape our shackles together

年方伯玉早，恨比四愁多。會待休車騎，相隨出罻羅。

....

NOTE: Tzu-hou was Liu Tsung-yuan's sobriquet. Concerning Ch'u Po-yu
蘧伯玉, Confucius once said, "When the Tao prevails in the state, he serves
in the government. When the Tao doesn't prevail, he retires and keeps his

views to himself" (*Analects* 15.6). According to Chuang-tzu, when Ch'u Po-yu turned sixty, he changed. He realized the views he had held were dependent on nothing more than his belief that they were right. Henceforth, he gave himself up to the mystery of doubt, as opposed to knowledge (*Chuangtzu* 25.8). Liu Yu-hsi was forty-five and Liu Tsung-yuan forty-three when this was written. The reference to "four sorrows" is to a poem with that title by Chang Heng 張衡 in which he expressed concerns that he and the one he loved were constantly being separated from each other, banished first to the east, then to the south, then to the west, and finally to the north. Although couched as a poem to a lover, it has long been interpreted as an official's plea for a closer relationship with his emperor.

102. ARRIVING AT CHIEHWEI WATERFALL AGAIN AND SPENDING THE NIGHT BELOW THE CLIFF

再至界圍巖水簾遂宿巖下

I thought we parted forever this spring
it's summer and I'm happy to see you again
everything that grows is in bloom
I think I'm in Hsuanpu Garden
suddenly it hails in tropical sunshine
it thunders and rains on a cloudless day
panpipe music rises from the pools
cranes strut and dance in the mist
tree limbs are wrapped in thick moss
plants are a wet iridescent green
rays of white light streak the sky
a cold glow gathers in the waves
scattered pearls shimmer in the depths
discarded pendants chime against the shore
the half-hidden cliff is a leaning painted screen
the new moon an ejected jade hook
the night is cool and stars fill the river
I feel like I'm sleeping in Tungfu Palace

發春念長違，中夏欣再覿。是時植物秀，杳若臨玄圃。
歊陽訝垂冰，白日驚雷雨。笙簧潭際起，鸑鶴雲間舞。
古苔凝青枝，陰草濕翠羽。蔽空素彩列，激浪寒光聚。
的皪沈珠淵，鏘鳴捐珮浦。幽巖畫屏倚，新月玉鉤吐。
夜涼星滿川，忽疑眠洞府。

....

NOTE: Written at the beginning of the fifth month of 815. Traveling to his new place of exile, Liu once more passes this waterfall between Hengyang and Yungchou that he passed three months earlier, an occasion he marked with poem 85. Hsuanpu Garden was located on one of the peaks in the Kunlun Mountains and was said to be the residence of Taoist immortals. The "scattered pearls" belong to those who have given up luxuries to follow the Taoist path. Likewise, the "discarded pendants" belong to officials who have left behind their badges of office. Hence, Liu sees everything here as indicative of the Taoist path, its rejection of the "hooks" of the world and its attainment of a realm beyond the mundane. Tungfu Palace was another celestial home of Taoists. (1147)

103. AT WANGCHIN POST STATION NORTH OF KUEICHOU, I CLEARED A TRAIL THROUGH THE BAMBOO TO A FISHING ROCK AND AM LEAVING THIS FOR HSU OF JUNGCHOU 桂州北望秦驛手開竹逕至釣磯留待徐容州

For whom did I clear this secluded path
for a friend coming here from the North
if your royal duties allow you time
try the top of Tzu-ling's boulder

幽徑為誰開，美人城北來。王程儻餘暇，一上子陵臺。

....

NOTE: Written in the fifth month of 815 in Kueichou. Liu was headed for his new place of exile in Liuchou and stopped in Kueichou (Kueilin) ahead of his friend Hsu Chun 徐俊, who was on his way to his new post in Jungchou 容州 (Junghsien 容縣), 200 kilometers beyond Liuchou. Hsu also appears in poem 110. Yen Tzu-ling 嚴子陵 was a recluse who turned down offers to serve at the Han-dynasty court of Emperor Kuang-wu 光武帝, preferring to fish from his boulder on the Fuchun River 富春江 south of Hangchou. When the emperor came to convince him to change his mind, Yen fell asleep with his feet stretched out on the emperor's stomach. Although Tzu-ling's boulder was still there when I visited in the 1990s, it has since disappeared under the waters of a dam. Liu's substitute boulder was somewhere on the upper stretch of the Kuei (or Li) River north of Kueichou. (1164)

104. Traveling by River in Lingnan 嶺南江行

Sailing south on infested waters into the land of mist
horizon of tanglehead stretching to the sea
hills marked by elephant swaths after a rain
dragon drool rising from the depths in the sun
poison-spitting frogs that can see a traveler's shadow
a typhoon sky frightening the passengers on board
my concerns however are other than these
namely how to bear white hair and the disappearing years

瘴江南去入雲煙，望盡黃茆是海遍。山腹雨晴添象跡，潭心日暖長蛟涎。
射工巧伺游人影，颶母偏驚旅客船。從此憂來非一事，豈容華髮待流年。

....

NOTE: Written in the sixth month of 815. Lingnan (South of the Ridges)
referred to the area south of the Nanling Mountains, basically what are the
provinces of Kuanghsi and Kuangtung. Bound for Liuchou, Liu was traveling
down the Kuei (or Li) River, along which hundreds of thousands, if not mil-
lions, of tourists travel every year to gaze upon the karst landscape through
which that river winds. "Dragon drool" refers to vapor rising from the river.
The Lingnan region was also known for a frog that lurked in streams and
spit sand at a person's shadow, whereupon that person dropped dead, or so
people claimed. The typhoon season in South China lasts from May through
October. The approach of one is often marked by unusual atmospheric phe-
nomena. The appearance of rainbows or crystalline skies devoid of moisture
is typical. (1168)

105. Sent to Family and Friends via a Fellow Bronze Fish Official on His Way to the Capital
銅魚使赴都寄親友

After traveling over mountains thousands of miles
I arrived to find this settlement deserted
such districts only get bronze fish officials
I won't be sending any more long-distance letters

行盡關山萬里餘，到時閭井是荒墟。附庸唯有銅魚使，此後無因寄遠書。

....

NOTE: Written in Liuchou at the end of the sixth month of 815 shortly after Liu arrived. This unnamed official heading back to Ch'ang-an was another local magistrate and thus carried a bronze fish as an emblem of office. Such officials were only allowed to send government-related correspondence with the regular courier service. Personal letters had to depend on the availability of friends or acquaintances. (1180)

106. CLIMBING LIUCHOU TOWER: SENT TO THE MAGISTRATES OF CHANG, TING, FENG, AND LIEN COUNTIES 登柳州城樓寄漳汀封連四州

The city tower here borders the wilderness
my cares are as endless as the ocean sky
a sudden wind churns the lotus-filled water
a downpour beats against the vine-covered wall
ridgetop trees block the distant views
the river's bends are as tortuous as my thoughts
since coming to this land of tattooed tribes
we share a realm beyond the reach of letters

城上高樓接大荒，海天愁思正茫茫。驚風亂颭芙蓉水，密雨斜侵薜荔墻。
嶺樹重遮千里目，江流曲似九回腸。共來百越文身地，猶自音書滯一鄉。

....

NOTE: Written in the early fall of 815. The four friends mentioned in the title were also exiled a second time to posts in South China for their involvement in the reform movement. Han T'ai 韓泰 and Han Yeh 韓曄 were banished to Fuchien province on the southeast coast: Han T'ai to Changchou and Han Yeh to Tingchou. Ch'en Lien 陳諫 and Liu Yu-hsi were banished to Kuangtung province: Ch'en Lien to Fengchou and Liu Yu-hsi to Lienchou. The tower looked south onto the Liuchiang River and the karst landscape beyond it. During the T'ang this was where the Kuanghsi Superintendent's Office 廣西提督衙署 was located. (1164)

107. Responding to Liu of Lienchou's Use of "Pang" 答劉連州邦字

A linked jade disk doesn't represent a pair
our tallies were split to govern minor districts
I sailed down the Li beneath broken clouds
then up the Hsun like an arrow
I carried a crossbow to frighten the apes
to keep mastiffs at bay I beat a drum at night
admiring the mountains near his post from a distance
Governor Hsieh merely looked out his window

連璧本難雙，分符刺小邦。崩雲下灘水，劈箭上潯江。
負弩啼寒狄，鳴枹驚夜狵，遙憐郡山好，謝守但臨窗。

....

NOTE: Written in Liuchou in the early fall of 815. Despite having no means to maintain regular correspondence with friends in the capital, Liu had no trouble staying in touch with his fellow exiles in the South. This poem is addressed to Liu Yu-hsi, who had been banished to Lienchou (*lien* 連: "linked"), 300 kilometers to the east. The character *pang* 邦 refers to an administrative unit, here a "district." Apparently, Liu Yu-hsi used this term in a letter, as it's not present in any of the poems he wrote in Lienchou. The term "linked jade disk" referred to a piece of jade with two holes of unequal size given to favorites of the court. The holes represented the sun and the moon. Liu uses the term here to emphasize his constant separation from his "linked" friend. Tallies were given to provincial officials, with half of each tally remaining at court for use in verifying documents. After the first couplet, Liu recounts events of his journey to his new post. Following his parting from Liu Yu-hsi in Hengyang, Liu Tsung-yuan followed the Hsiang to its headwaters near Kueilin. Then from Kueilin he sailed down the Li (or Kuei) River to Wuchou and up the Hsun and Liuchiang Rivers to Liuchou. The normal water route between Kueilin and Liuchou was the Loching River, which was reached via the Hsiangssu Canal 相思渠 just south of Kueilin. That route was a distance of 120 kilometers. The route Liu outlines here was over 600 kilometers. Obviously, he wasn't in a hurry and must have heard about the scenery along the Li. At the end of this poem, Liu reminds his friend that Hsieh An 謝安 (320–385) was content to admire the peaks surrounding his various posts and focused on his work instead. It was not until he was in his forties that Hsieh finally accepted a position. Both men were in their forties when Tsung-yuan wrote this. (1168)

108. THE HILL TRIBES OF LIUCHOU 柳州峒氓

People south of town have to ford the river
with different clothes and speech they're hard to get to know
they wrap salt in bamboo leaves to take back to the hills
and wrap rice in lily pads to eat on market days
they make goose-feather quilts to protect against the cold
and tell the future with chicken bones and worship water spirits
at court it's such a bother talking through interpreters
I'd like to toss my hat away and get a few tattoos

郡城南下接通津，異服殊音不可親。青箬裹鹽歸峒客，綠荷包飯趁虛人。
鵝毛御臘縫山罽，雞骨占年拜水神。愁向公庭問重譯，欲投章甫作文身。

....

NOTE: Written in Liuchou in the fall of 815. Han Chinese were in the minority in the Liuchou region—and still are. More than half the current population of Liuchou county belongs to such ethnic groups as the Chuang, the Miao, the Yao, and the Tung. Officials were required to wear a ceremonial hat when performing public functions, and educated Chinese usually felt undressed without something, even something as simple as a bandanna, covering their head. (1169)

109. Planting White *Zingiber* 種白蘘荷

"Toxins are made from a pot full of bugs"
the locals here have lots of myths
all more or less concern poison
like "those who chase wealth aren't kind"
"my produce comes from afar"
or "the wine in your cup is aged"
sweet words mask something bitter
how do we know they're true
platitudes are affectations
they make a northerner cringe
"coins" I'll admit "buy harm"
but hunger makes living hard
and exile means living in fear
and thinking of the past only adds to one's grief
but people here have this magical plant
they no longer pray to the gods
in the Fire Emperor's book of wonders
this one it says is especially prized
found along high mountain trails
it has helped restore my health
thriving in dark shady places
it's something I love to see

皿蟲化為癘，夷俗多所神。銜猜每臘毒，謀富不為仁。
蔬果自遠至，盃酒盈肆陳。言甘中必苦，何用知其真。
華潔事外飾，尤病中州人。錢刀恐賈害，飢至益逡巡。
竄伏常戰慄，懷故逾悲辛。庶氏有嘉草，攻檜事久泯。
炎帝垂靈編，言此殊足珍。崎嶇乃有得，託以全余身。
紛敷碧樹陰，眄睞心所親。

....

Note: Written in Liuchou most likely in 815. *Zingiber striolatum* is meant.
A member of the ginger family, its rhizomes are a delicacy. The hill tribes of
the Liuchou region believed if they put a bunch of bugs in a pot for a year,

the one that survived would be more lethal than the rest and could be used to make the most toxic of poisons. The fourth line is quoted from *Mencius* (3B.3.5): "Yang Hu says, 'Whoever is concerned with wealth isn't kind. Whoever is concerned with kindness isn't rich.'" The other sayings are similar, but I have no idea who coined them. Having quoted several, Liu then adds his own. The Fire Emperor was Shen Nung 神農 (ca. 2500 BC), who authored China's first pharmacopoeia listing all known plants, minerals, and animals with medicinal uses. *Zingiber* is used to promote blood circulation, reduce inflammation, and eliminate toxins, among many other things In Liu's case, he sees in it possible relief for indecisiveness, anxiety, and distress. This is not just a poem about medicinal plants. (1227)

110. Sent in Reply to Palace Aide Hsu Er about Events at the Lakeside Inn in Puning

酬徐二中丞普寧郡內池館即事見寄

I recall the old columns of palace geese
the empty halls facing sweet-scented ponds
the setting sun lighting red pillars
the profusion of flowers reflected in our cups
streams here are closer to the sea
and the trees on these mountains are taller
having shared the burdens of honor and disgrace
let's plan to meet back home

鵁鴻念舊行，虛館對芳塘。落日明朱檻，繁花照羽觴。
泉歸滄海近，樹入楚山長。榮賤俱為累，相期在故鄉。

....

NOTE: Written in Liuchou in 815. Puning was 200 kilometers southeast of
Liuchou. It was the region's administrative center, while nearby Jungchou
容州 was its military center—not the same Jungchou 融州, as in poem 134.
Hsu Er, or Hsu Chun, who also appears in poem 103, was sent to Jungchou
as military commissioner but here retains the previous title he held at court.
Liu doesn't tell us about the events his friend wrote about, but he tries to
put their shared past and present in a rosy light and hope for the best in the
future. (1170)

111. After Critiquing Yin Hsien's Calligraphy in Jest, I Send This to Liu of Lienchou and Also Share It with His Two Students, Meng and Lun
殷賢戲批書後寄劉連州并示孟崙二童

I thought I would send Yu An-hsi my work
on the back I should have added an inscription
his students I have recently heard
are bored at their inkwells with the family chicken

書成欲寄庾安西，紙背應勞手自題。聞道近來諸子弟，臨池尋已厭家雞。

....

NOTE: Written in Liuchou in the fall of 815. This marked the first of a series of poems Liu exchanged with his friend Liu Yu-hsi on the subject of calligraphy. Like Liu Tsung-yuan, Liu Yu-hsi was also exiled farther south than before—in his case, all the way to Lienchou, just inside neighboring Kuangtung province to the east. Yin Hsien was one of Liu Yu-hsi's students and came to Liu Tsung-yuan for instruction in calligraphy. Liu Tsung-yuan uses the name of Yu An-hsi here in place of his exiled friend's. Yu was a famous artist of the fifth century on whose paintings the famous calligrapher Wang Hsi-chih 王羲之 wrote inscriptions. In Chinese, "family chicken" is a critical reference to a school of calligraphy as tantamount to chicken scratching. Liu Yu-hsi wrote the following poem in reply. (1175)

In Thanks for Liu of Liuchou's Gift of His Family Chicken 酬柳柳州家雞之贈 by Liu Yu-hsi

Every day at their inkwells my chickens scratch away
I've been thinking of writing an essay for Kuan-nu
Mister Liu's new style is the talk of the age
my ginger-shoot fingers are clasped in vain

日日臨池弄小雞，還思寫論付官奴。柳家新樣元和腳，且盡薑芽斂手徒。

....

NOTE: Written in Lienchou by Liu Yu-hsi in the fall of 815. Kuan-nu was the name of the daughter of the famous calligrapher Wang Hsi-chih, who once wrote an essay on calligraphy for her. Liu Yu-hsi, however, is using Wang's daughter to refer to Liu Tsung-yuan's daughter, who would have been four at this time. Liu Tsung-yuan's first daughter, born in Ch'ang-an in 801, died in Yungchou in 810. His second daughter was born in Yungchou the following year. The Chinese name of the reign period is used in the third line. The Yuanho period began in 805 when both men were exiled. In the last line, Liu describes his futile bow of admiration with his fingers interlocked. (1176)

112–113. ANOTHER GIFT: TWO POEMS 重贈二首

ONE

As for the chickens you've led to the inkwell
your students still have conflicting views
they've come to my hole-in-the-wall now with questions
my standard response is How would I know

聞說將雛向墨池，劉家還有異同詞。如今試遣隈牆問，已道世人那得知。

TWO

No one really knows what's right
ginger shoots often come with a grimace
if you thought my school didn't have any students
why did you ask for a sample last year

世上悠悠不識真，薑芽盡是捧心人。若道柳家無子弟，往年何事乞西賓。

....

NOTE: Written in Liuchou in the fall of 815. Ginger shoots refer to the appear-
ance of a person's fingers when they're interlocked in a bow of respect, which
Liu Tsung-yuan describes as a bit excessive, if not forced. The sample most
likely refers to Liu Yu-hsi's request for Liu Tsung-yuan to write out Pan Ku's
班固 "Ode to the Western Capital" 西都賦. (1177)

IN REPLY TO YOUR FIRST PIECE 答前篇 BY LIU YU-HSI

I can't scold the kids when they play with their brushes
when they splash mud on jade I still praise their effort
I heard you're not done dreaming of bears
which of your daughters is Madame Wei

小兒弄筆不能嗔，涴壁書牎且賞勤。聞彼夢熊猶未兆，女中誰是衛夫人。

NOTE: The young son of the famous calligrapher Wang Hsi-chih was noted for writing with mud on anything he could find, including pieces of jade, even window screens. In the third line, Liu Yu-hsi is refering to a couplet from a poem in the Book of Poetry: "A bear, indeed a bear / the blessing of a son" 維熊維熊，南子之祥. Apparently, Tsung-yuan confided to his friend that he was still hoping for a son. The last line, though, is a bit curious, as surely Liu Yu-hsi knew that his friend had only one daughter at this time (see poem 114) and that his older daughter had died five years earlier. Or maybe he knew something Liu Tsung-yuan's biographers didn't know. Madame Wei refers to Wei Shuo 衛鑠, the woman who taught Wang Hsi-chih calligraphy when he was a child. (1178)

IN REPLY TO YOUR SECOND PIECE 答後篇 BY LIU YU-HSI

They recently managed to record their names
copying the "Western Capital" is out of the question
but lately they've shown more interest in their inkwells
tell Yuan-ch'ang they're ready for straight lines

昔日慵工記姓名，遠勞辛苦寫西京。近來漸有臨池興，為報元常欲抗行。

NOTE: In the second line, Liu is referring to his earlier request for Liu Tsung-yuan to copy Pan Ku's "Ode to the Western Capital" for him. As for the reference in the last line, Wang Hsi-chih once compared his straight lines with those of Chung Yao 鍾繇 (whose sobriquet was Yuan-ch'ang) and his slanting lines with those of Chang Chih 張芝. Chung was known for the more controlled lines of the *k'ai-shu* (regular) and *li-shu* (archaic) styles, while Chang was famous for the free-form of his *ts'ao-shu* (grass) style. (1179)

114. Before the Exchange 疊前

Your students have lately been splashing in inkwells
I admire these branches of your jewel-encrusted tree
playing with clay here is only my princess
outside in the yard I see nothing but bird tracks

小學新翻墨沼波，羨君瓊樹散枝柯。在家弄土唯嬌女，空覺庭前鳥跡多。

....

NOTE: Written in Liuchou in the fall of 815 in response to Liu Yu-hsi's
response. In the third line, playing with clay or pottery shards was a euphe-
mism for a daughter, while the phrase "playing with jade" was a common
reference to a son. Liu didn't have a son until the following year. (1179)

115. After the Exchange 疊後

Our careers were failures unlike our shameful art
our names were linked with our South Palace drafts
I urge you to hurry and add to your skills
let's be like those two famous scribes of the past

事業無成恥藝成，南宮起草舊連名。勸君火急添功用，趁取當時二妙聲。

....

NOTE: Written in Liuchou in the fall of 815. "Shameful art" refers to writing drafts of little more than bureaucratic significance. South Palace was the location of, and thus another name for, the Department of State Affairs, which was in charge of drafting documents. While both men previously held lesser posts, at the time of their exile, Liu Tsung-yuan was serving as vice director of the Ministry of Rites, and Liu Yu-hsi as vice director of the State Farm Bureau, both of which were part of the Department of State Affairs. The last line refers to a time in the third century when the Department of State Affairs was headed by Wei Kuan 衛瓘 and Suo Ching 索靖, two men famous for their calligraphy, who rose to even higher posts. (1180)

116–117. Two Poems Presented in Reply to Hermit Chia P'eng Who Has Been Enjoying Himself Recently Planting Pine Trees in the Prefecture

酬賈鵬山人郡內新栽松寓興見贈二首

One

Flowering and decay naturally differ
not minding is its greatest achievement
its blooms are so soft in the sunlight
their radiance eases hard times
a pine tree no one noticed in the gorge
is flourishing now in my yard
displaying its beauty in the snow
its winter inflorescence complementing its green
having long admired its detachment
I'm using it to invite purer air

芳朽自為別，無心乃玄功。夭夭日放花，榮耀將安窮。
青松遭澗底，擢蒔茲庭中。積雪表明秀，寒花助葱蘢。
幽貞夙有慕，持以延清風。

Two

You couldn't stay in hiding forever
ironically your stillness made you known
you looked so strange coming down the mountain
now you resemble everyone else
but with a vitality that remains unchanged
and a mind that outshines us all
how do you endure the vulgarity and the noise
I was never very good at acceptance
from your flute and zither come the purest notes
in tune with the sound of this breeze

無能常閉閣，偶以靜見名。奇姿來遠山，忽似人家生。
勁色不改舊，芳心與誰榮。喧卑豈所安，任物非我情。
清韻動竽瑟，諧此風中聲。

....

NOTE: Written in Liuchou in the winter of 815. Liu wrote these two poems in reply to a hermit named Chia P'eng 賈鵬 who sent him a poem titled "Enjoying Myself Recently by Planting Pine Trees in the Prefecture," which has been lost. (1170)

118. Presented in the Rain to Hermit Chia of Immortal Peak 雨中贈仙人山賈山人

Last night a winter rain poured on the river
this morning the clouds hid Immortal Peak
I'm guessing that panther is up there somewhere
laughing at you stuck down here in the mud

寒江夜雨聲潺潺，曉雲遮盡仙人山。遙知玄豹在深處，下笑羈絆泥塗間。

....

Note: Written in Liuchou in the winter of 815. Chia P'eng also appears in the previous two poems. Apparently, he decided to spend some time in town—not a bad idea in winter. The hermit Han-shan 寒山 (ca. 800) abandoned his cave and spent winters in a monastery. (1172)

119–120. In Reply to Han of Changchou's Letter Announcing the Death of Master Ch'e, I Send Two Quatrains 韓漳州書報徹上人亡因寄二絕

ONE

I heard his Yueh dialect in the capital as a boy
even people from there found it hard to understand
when he painted that gathering at Orchid Pavilion
he left out Master Tao-lin

早歲京華聽越吟，聞君江海分逾深。他時若寫蘭亭會，莫畫高僧支道林。

TWO

Taking his precious book from its sleeve once again
I stood in the autumn wind and intoned the lines he left
if the rivers of Kuci flow a thousand *li* a day
how long will these tears take to reach Yungtung

頻把瓊書出袖中，獨吟遺句立秋風。桂江日夜流千里，揮淚何時到甬東。

....

NOTE: Written in Liuchou in the winter of 815. The Buddhist monk Ling-ch'e 靈徹 died that fall in Hsuanchou 宣州 at the age of seventy-one. Han T'ai was one of the eight men banished, together with Liu, as a result of the failed reform movement. In Han's case, he was banished to Changchou 漳州 in Fuchien province.

ONE: Master Ch'e was from Shaohsing, the capital of the ancient state of Yueh, and was a well-known poet and painter. Lanting 蘭亭 (Orchid Pavilion) was just outside Shaohsing and was made famous by a gathering attended by the calligrapher Wang Hsi-chih (303–361) and his friends, which included Chih Tao-lin (314–366). Tao-lin (aka Chih Tun 支遁) was one of the most famous monks of his day and known for his expositions of Buddhist, Taoist, and Confucian doctrines. Among his more widely circulated statements was "all appearances are empty"—hence, Ling-ch'e's decision to omit him from the painting.

Two: Ling-ch'e wrote more than 2,000 poems, but only two dozen survive. Poets often sent copies of their poems to friends. Sometimes they even sent bound collections, which would be kept in protective sleeves. The rivers of the Kuei region, which include the Liuchiang River, empty into the West River, which empties into the South China Sea near Hong Kong. The Yungtung Islands (nowadays known as the Choushan Islands 舟山群島) are in the East China Sea and were part of Ling-che's home state of Yueh. The distance from Liuchou by water would be about 4,000 *li,* or 2,000 kilometers. (1181)

121. Impromptu Poem on the Falling of Banyan Leaves in the Second Month in Liuchou
柳州二月榕葉落盡偶題

As a failure and a stranger I'm equally depressed
with spring resembling fall I'm also confused
when it rains in this hill town all the flowers disappear
banyan leaves cover the ground and the orioles can't stop singing

宦情羈思共悽悽，春半如秋意轉迷。山城過雨百花盡，榕葉滿庭鶯亂啼。

....

NOTE: Written in Liuchou in the spring of 816. Rains here are not as gentle as they are in Yungchou. Banyans in this part of China lose their leaves in spring rather than autumn, but that doesn't seem to bother the orioles. (1172)

122. Parting from My Cousin Tsung-yi 別舍弟宗一

Lifeless and depressed my spirit is doubly dark
parting at the river our tears overflow
banished from the capital 2,000 miles from home
I've died a million times these twelve years in the wilds
the miasmic clouds of Kueiling are like ink
Tungting Lake in late spring merges with the sky
I imagine when I meet you hereafter in my dreams
it will be in Chingmen in the mist-filled woods of Ying

零落殘魂倍黯然，雙垂別淚越江邊。一身去國六千里，萬死投荒十二年。
桂嶺瘴來雲似墨，洞庭春盡水如天。欲知此後相思夢，長在荊門郢樹煙。

....

NOTE: Written in Liuchou in the late spring or early summer of 816. Liuchou
was located in a mountainous region known as Kuei, or Kueiling—refer-
ring to the ridges (*ling*) of Kuei. After accompanying Liu to Liuchou, his
cousin Liu Tsung-yi 柳宗一 headed back to the Yangtze via Tungting Lake,
which becomes shallow in winter but fills up again in spring to become one
of China's largest freshwater lakes. Liu's cousin's route would have taken him
down the Hsiang River, across Tungting Lake, and finally across the Yangtze.
Chingchou was on the Yangtze's north shore. Just north of the city was where
the ancient Ch'u capital of Ying 郢 and its fabled woods were located. The
appearance of Chingmen 荊門 in the text is probably a mistake for Ching-
chou, as it was another 90 kilometers north of Chingchou. Another cousin,
Liu Tsung-chih, also accompanied Liu to Liuchou but died a month after
arriving. Hence, Liu's spirit is "doubly dark." (1173)

123. Using the Rhyme in Elder Chou Twenty-Two's Reply to the Magistrate of Chenchou's "Anchored at Night in Hengchou" about Receiving a Letter from Shaochou Along with a Locally Produced Yellow Tea, I Have Dashed This Off in Reply to Express My Thoughts 奉和周二十二丈酬郴州侍郎衡江夜泊得韶州書并附當州生黃茶一封率然成篇代意之作

These hills and peaks welcome the light of your virtue
your journey from Heaven is finally over
the three knives in your dream happily aren't far off
but the five years in your letter sounds excessive
as the river moon sets I think about you more
as the ridge clouds depart so do my thoughts
let's meet at the minister's office
let's invite Mister Chou too

丘山仰德耀，天路下征騑。夢喜三刀近，書嫌五載違。
凝情江月落，屬思嶺雲飛。會入司徒府，還邀周掾歸。

....

NOTE: Written in Liuchou the summer of 816, to and about Liu's fellow exiles. Chou was serving as magistrate of Shaochou (Shaokuan in Kuangtung province) and sent a letter to Yang Yu-ling, who had been exiled and was on his way to his post as magistrate of Chenchou. "Heaven" here refers to the capital. Yang also appears in poems 124, 128, and 129 and Chou in poem 126. The third-century general Wang Chun 王濬 once dreamed there were three knives hanging over his bed, then dreamed that a fourth was added. His assistant dismissed his worries and said three knives resembled the character *chou* 州 for "district," and the character for "add" was *yi* 益, suggesting Wang was about to be appointed governor of Yi District 益州 in North China. Sure enough, that was what happened. The standard period of exile was either two or five years. Unlike for Liu, in Yang's case it turned out to be two. Once recalled, he rose to lead a number of government agencies. Yang was a vice director in the Ministry of Personnel prior to his exile (and is so called in poem 129), but Liu elevates him here to "minister." Liu's hope is for them all to meet back in Ch'ang-an. (1174)

124. Imperial Secretary Yang Sent a Calligraphy Brush from Chenchou Similar to One I Used as a Boy. As It Caused Me to Reconsider His Achievements, I Offer Some Longer Lines
楊尚書寄郴筆知是小生本樣令更商攤使盡其功輒獻長句

A pointed awl that carves jade into art
a fog-filled cloud that has reached the South Seas
used by the royal secretary and drafter of decrees
and now by this scribe to copy the *Taoteching*
how do these higher arts help us get ahead
a few subtle words can spread such sweet perfume
while your ministerial moon shines upon Kueiyang
this brush tip shall channel the rabbit in the sky

截玉銛錐作妙形，貯雲含霧到南溟。尚書舊用裁天詔，內史新將寫道經。
曲藝豈能裨損益，微辭祇欲播芳馨。桂陽卿月光輝徧，毫末應傳顧兔靈。

....

NOTE: Written in Liuchou in the summer of 816. Yang Yu-ling was one of Liu's oldest friends, and the two exchanged poems as well as letters. In the midst of an otherwise successful career at court, Yang was banished in the fourth month of 816 to serve as magistrate of Chenchou, 150 kilometers south of Hengyang and 500 kilometers northeast of where Liu was serving. Kuei-yang was the name of the administrative region that included Chenchou, Hengyang, and Yungchou, Liu's former post. Yang would be recalled two years later to head the Ministry of Rites. The metaphors of the first two lines refer to the calligraphy brush. A sharpened awl is easy to imagine, but the fog/cloud image is less obvious. It refers to a calligraphy brush once it's been dipped in ink. Liu's post was sufficiently distant from the capital that people thought of it as at the edge of the South China Sea, which was actually another 350 kilometers away. After receiving this particular brush, Liu used it to write out Lao-tzu's *Taoteching*—a text in which the new moon is frequently used as a symbol for the Tao. Presumably, he sent the finished work to Yang, as Liu's calligraphy was prized by friends and collectors. The rabbit in the last line refers to one that lives on that celestial orb. Hence, it's also a metaphor for the moon. Then, too, calligraphy brushes were often made with rabbit fur. The "longer lines" in the title refer to a poem of seven-character lines, as opposed to lines of five characters. (1145)

125. Planting Tree Orchids 種木槲花

Every year I caught glimpses of the royal garden
I find myself now at the farthest edge of Heaven
since I'll be serving in Dragon Town awhile
I'm planting orchids in my yard wherever I can

上苑年年占物華，飄零今日在天涯。祇因長作龍城守，剩種庭前木槲花。

....

NOTE: Written in Liuchou, also known as Lungcheng 龍城 (Dragon Town), in the summer of 816. These particular orchids are also known as tree orchids, as they normally grow on oaks. Until recently, some of the hill tribes in this part of China grew them on their wood-shingled roofs. In the first line, Liu mentions the Shangyuan Garden by name. This "garden" was actually a series of parks established in the Ch'in dynasty and expanded during the Han. It stretched for over a hundred kilometers west of Ch'ang-an. Here "Heaven" refers to the limits of imperial control: namely, the empire. (1185)

126. SENT FROM LIUCHOU TO ELDER CHOU OF SHAOCHOU 柳州寄丈人周韶州

In this remote outpost amid thousands of peaks
the office is silent long before sunset
official seals mildew from weeks without use
inkstones spend days in dust-covered cases
in Meiling's cooler mists kingfishers hide
in Kuei's autumn waters snapping turtles thrive
the Elder gave up state affairs long ago
imagine how haggard I've become this year

越絕孤城千萬峰，空齋不語坐高春。印文生綠經旬合，硯匣留塵盡日封。
梅嶺寒煙藏翡翠，桂江秋水露鼩鰡。丈人本自忘機事，為想年來憔悴容。

....

NOTE: Written in Liuchou in the fall of 816. Chou Chun-ch'ao 周君巢 was an older man with an interest in Taoist practice; he was serving as magistrate of Shaochou (Shaokuan), 500 kilometers to the east in neighboring Kuangtung province. Earlier, when Liu was serving in Yungchou, Chou wrote to him inquiring about the availability of ingredients for elixirs. Liu wrote back poking fun at Chou's pursuit of longevity. Despite such differences, they remained on good terms, and Liu pokes fun at Chou here too by contrasting his own place of exile with his friend's. On his way to Shaochou, Liu's friend traveled south from the Yangtze via the Kan River and then over Meiling Pass 梅嶺關 (Plum Ridge), also known as Tayuling Pass 大庾嶺 (Tayu Ridge), into Kuangtung. Kueichou was not only the old name of the town Kueilin but also of the region that included both it and Liuchou. Hence, all the rivers were in "the land of Kuei." Documents were stamped with red seals to make them official, and inkstones used for grinding ink were kept in wooden cases to keep away dust and to prevent leftover ink from drying out too quickly. After describing his new place of work, Liu contrasts his friend's place of exile beyond Meiling Pass with his more inhospitable world and his friend's acceptance of his assignment with his own distress at having recently returned to the capital only to be banished to an even more distant post. (1165)

127. Having Received a Letter from Lu of Hengchou, I'm Sending Back a Poem 得盧衡州書因以詩寄

Stop sighing as if Lincheng were in the tropics
the odd column of geese still announces fall
these east-facing mountains in Linyi are like spears
and the south-flowing waters of the Tsangke like soup
meanwhile autumn fog envelops your swaying reeds
and sunsets illuminate your dangling oranges
not being an exile among islands of duckweed
I send these thoughts to the Hsiang from far away

臨蒸且莫歎炎方，為報秋來鴈幾行。林邑東迴山似戟，牂牁南下水如湯。
兼葭淅瀝含秋霧，橘柚玲瓏透夕陽。非是白蘋洲畔客，還將遠意問瀟湘。

....

NOTE: Written in Liuchou in the fall of 816 in reply to a man serving as the magistrate of Hengchou (Hengyang). As in the previous poem, Liu contrasts the downside of his own place of exile with his friend's. This Lu of Hengchou was not the same Lu of Hengchou in poems 67 and 79. Although both served as the same town's magistrate, the characters for their family names are different. Lincheng 臨蒸 (Overlooking the Cheng) was an old name for Hengchou, as the town is situated where the Cheng River 蒸江 joins the Hsiang. It was located more than three degrees north of the Tropic of Cancer, while Liuchou was only one degree, which can make a big difference when it comes to weather patterns. Hengchou (or Lincheng) was reportedly as far south as geese migrated. Liuchou was beyond their range. Linyi was the name of a kingdom and later an administrative area of Vietnam. Liu uses the term here to emphasize the remoteness of his post. The Tsangke 牂牁 is an old name for the Liuchiang River that flows through Liuchou. The last couplet borrows heavily from "South of the Yangtze" 江南曲, a song by Liu Yun 柳惲, a fifth-century exile serving near the "islands and duckweed" of Tungting Lake, not far north of where the recipient of this poem was serving. (1167)

128. Sent to Elder Yang on Hearing of the Death of Master Ch'e 聞徹上人亡寄侍郎楊丈

The great monk from Yueh whose surname was T'ang
how often we heard his belt pendants chime
what happened to those flowers once they fell from the sky
who'll gather their golden petals for the vice director now

東越高僧還姓湯，幾時瓊珮觸鳴瑙。空花一散不知處，誰采金英與侍郎。

....

NOTE: Written in Liuchou in the winter of 816. The recipient of this poem was Yang Yu-ling, who was serving as magistrate of Chenchou. As in poems 119 and 120, the monk Ling-ch'e is meant. Before he became a monk, Ling-ch'e's name was T'ang Ch'eng-yuan 湯澄源. He was a native of Shaohsing in what was once the ancient state of Yueh. Ling-ch'e had the same surname as the Buddhist monk Hui-lin 惠林, who had a similar close relationship with a poet, namely Pao Chao 鮑照 (414–466). Hui-lin once sent Pao a poem about golden petals in the sky. Such metaphors were a common way for Buddhists to describe objects in the material world we normally think of as real. Master Ch'e was a minor celebrity in Ch'ang-an, before being banished from the capital for "spreading rumors." While he was there, he knew both Liu and Yang. Out of politeness, Liu uses the title of Yang's previous post in the last line, a title he shared with the earlier poet, Pao Chao. (1183)

129. MATCHING VICE DIRECTOR YANG OF CHENCHOU WHO MATCHED FORMER VICE DIRECTOR LI'S "TEN COUPLETS ON CLIMBING NORTH TOWER ON A SUMMER DAY," USING THE SAME RHYME
奉和楊尚書郴州追和故李中書夏日登北樓十韻之作依本詩韻次用

At the city tower someone left a song
new rhymes worth gold in the South
the scene had to do with searching for the Way
someone hoping to find a forgotten dream
he was standing at the railing above the summer heat
trying to see something in the distant wilds
the phoenix is gone but not his fine lines
the perfume of his thoughts lingers on
a dragon swam out of the deep
a crane called circling a peak
wind stirs waves on the Hsiang
clouds create ten thousand miles of shade
his example was equal to any in the realm
his duckweed bouquets rivalled those at court
his serenity dispelled the cares of others
his hospitable ways made visitors stay longer
he was a great steed that could run forever
but don't get those cuckoos started
climbing up here today
I hear someone singing that Farmer Liang song

郡樓有遺唱，新和敵南金。境以道情得，人期幽夢尋。
層軒隔炎署，迥野恣窺臨。鳳去徽音續，芝焚芳意深。
游鱗出陷浦，唳鶴繞仙岑。風起三湘浪，雲生萬里陰。
宏規齊德宇，麗藻競詞林。靜契分憂術，閑同遲客心。
驊騮當遠步，鶗鴂莫相侵。今日登高處，還聞梁父吟。

NOTE: Written in Liuchou in 816. After reading a poem by a recently deceased colleague, and another by a friend that matched its rhyme scheme, Liu imagines himself where both poems were written, in Chenchou. Yang Yu-ling was demoted from his post as vice director of the Ministry of Revenue in the fourth month of 816 and exiled to Chenchou to serve as its new magistrate. Following his arrival a month or so later, he wrote a poem in which he matched the rhyme scheme of Li Chi-fu 李吉甫, who had written a poem of ten couplets during his time as magistrate of Chenchou a dozen years earlier. After Li was recalled, he rose to become one of the most powerful officials at court. He died in the winter of 814. Liu and Yang both knew him. The phoenix refers to Li, and the perfumed lines to the poem he wrote on North Tower. Liu mentions in passing two of the stories associated with Chenchou. The first concerns the dragon daughter of the King of Tungting Lake, who was rescued from her wicked husband by the scholar Liu Yi 柳毅. The second refers to the Taoist healer Su Tan 蘇耽, who once lived on Chenchou's sacred peak of Malingshan 馬嶺山, across the lake from North Tower. Liu then looks for an appropriate metaphor for the departed magistrate. The duckwood bouquets refer to the poems of someone living in exile and the cuckoos to the instigators of court gossip. Finally, the song about farmers refers to one composed by the famous third-century recluse Chu-ke Liang 諸葛亮, who was often heard singing it. Once he was called out of his self-imposed retirement, he became one of the great military tacticians in Chinese history. (1143)

130. Written in Reply to Master Hao-ch'u Who Sent a Quatrain about Climbing Immortal Peak
浩初上人見貽絕句欲登仙人山因以酬之

The jeweled trees are chiming on that slope across the river
but illness has restricted my transcendent travels
the realms of immortals aren't part of my mandate
I trust your jangling staff will carry you into the void

珠樹玲瓏隔翠微，病來方外事多違。仙山不屬分符客，一任凌空錫杖飛。

....

NOTE: Written in Liuchou in 817. Looking south across the Liuchiang River from Liuchou, Liu sees the karst peak of Hsienjenshan (Immortal Mountain), which rises 270 meters above the river. Nowadays it's called Ma-anshan 馬鞍山 (Saddle Mountain). It's a good thirty-minute hike from the foot to the top, assuming one doesn't stop to enjoy the view along the way. Two of the Eight Immortals are said to have spent time in its rocky recesses, and it was also visited by the travel writer Hsu Hsia-k'o 徐霞客 in the Ming dynasty. Peaks where immortals live are often described as covered by jeweled trees and flowers. And why wouldn't they be? Hao-ch'u 浩初, however, wasn't a Taoist. He was a Buddhist monk from Changsha who exchanged poems with both Liu Yu-hsi and Liu Tsung-yuan. He also appears in poem 133. When hiking on mountain trails, monks often carry a staff with tin rings on top that jangle to warn animals of their approach. (1172)

131. Sent in Reply to Censor Ts'ao on Passing Through Hsiang County 酬曹侍御過象縣見寄

On that jade-green stream below Cracked Head Mountain
a poet in his magnolia boat is serving far from home
the spring wind stirs endless thoughts of the Hsiao and Hsiang
I would pick you some duckweed flowers but can't get free

破額山前碧玉流，騷人遙駐木蘭舟。春風無限瀟湘意，欲採蘋花不自由。

....

NOTE: Written in Liuchou most likely in 817. Liu's friend was posted to tour the areas under the administrative control of Liuchou, of which Liu was the magistrate, and to report to the court on whether officials were following imperial protocol. Hsiang county 象縣 was to the southeast, not far down the Liuchiang River from where Liu was serving. Nowadays it's called Paisha county 白沙鄉. A "magnolia boat" originally referred to a vessel made of magnolia wood, but the term came to refer to any handsome craft, especially one that carried a poet. In the last couplet, Liu recalls the ten springs he witnessed on the Hsiao and Hsiang Rivers while living in Yungchou. Presumably the two men met during that time. Duckweed is an aquatic plant and often used in Chinese poetry as a metaphor for the rootless life of exile. In Yungchou, Liu had no duties and went hiking or boating at the slightest provocation, but in Liuchou he had a job. (1186)

132. Picking Cherries and Presenting Them First to Layman Yuan and Later to Taoist Master Chu at Looking for Immortals Pavilion on South Tower 摘櫻桃贈元居士時在望仙亭南樓與朱道士同處

These red fruits from across the sea are for those in my thoughts
I'm at the tower again looking for immortals
if a winged traveler from Penglai should ever visit
I'm not some little scamp who steals peaches

海上朱櫻贈所思，樓居況是望仙時。蓬萊羽客如相訪，不是偷桃一小兒。

....

NOTE: Written in Liuchou most likely in the summer of 817. Directly across the Liuchiang River from the pavilion on Liuchou's South Tower was Immortal Peak (Hsienjenshan). The cherry arrived in China from India but didn't make much of an impact until modern times. The name the Chinese gave it means "baby peach"—the peach being the fruit most associated with immortality. Penglai Island 蓬萊岛 was said to be somewhere off the coast of Shantung province and was one of the more famous homes of immortals. In the last line, Liu refers to the story of Tung-fang Shuo 束方朔, who stole some of the peaches Taoism's Queen Mother of the West 西王母 intended to give Emperor Wu of the Han dynasty 漢武帝. In this case, Liu disavows any such interest. (1185)

133. With Master Hao-ch'u Looking at Mountains: Sent to Loved Ones back in the Capital

與浩初上人同看山寄京華親故

These peaks at the ocean's edge are like knives
they've cut my aching heart to pieces this fall
if I could conjure a million bodies
from every summit I would look for my hometown

海畔尖山似劍鋩，秋來處處割愁腸。若為化得身千億，散上峰頭望故鄉。

....

NOTE: Written in Liuchou in fall 817 when the Buddhist monk Hao-ch'u visited. Liu met Hao-ch'u in Changsha on his way into exile. Hao-ch'u was a disciple of the Zen master Lung An-hai 龍安海, whose epitaph Hao-ch'u had asked Liu to write in 808. Liu's new place of exile was surrounded by the same kind of karst peaks Kueilin is known for. As far as people back in the capital would have been concerned, it was sufficiently far away to be at the "ocean's edge." In the first chapter of the *Lankavatara Sutra,* the Buddha manifests countless bodies on countless peaks to teach different audiences the Dharma. Liu tells his monk friend if he were capable of such a feat, he would give his manifestations a different mission. (1146)

134. CLIMBING LIUCHOU'S OSHAN MOUNTAIN 登柳州峨山

Up a deserted mountain one fall day at noon
I climbed alone thinking distant thoughts
I wish I could see my hometown
there's Jungchou to the northwest

荒山秋日午，獨上意悠悠。如何望鄉處，西北是融州。

....

NOTE: Written in Liuchou in the fall of 817. Oshan is the name of a peak in the
western part of the city—just beyond what is now the Liuchou train station.
Like Hsienjenshan, it's about thirty minutes from the foot to the summit—
but it's a steep climb and requires pulling oneself up in places by using iron
chains placed along the trail for that purpose. A longer, easier route up the
opposite side takes about an hour. Both trails lead to a lookout platform on
top. Unfortunately, a weather station now blocks the view to the northwest.
This Jungchou—not to be confused with Jungchou 容州, 200 kilometers to the
southeast, where Liu's friend in poem 103 was posted—was 80 kilometers to
the north, while Liu's hometown of Ch'ang-an was another 1,000 kilometers
beyond that. (1166)

135. To Wei Heng 寄韋珩

I left for Liuchou through the eastern suburbs
seeing me off were the worthiest of men
dazzled by the sight of such uncommon gems
I journeyed into the wilds and a different realm
summer heat and air made it hard to breathe
I couldn't stop panting and gasping
from Kueichou southwest it was a thousand more *li*
I sailed down the Li past neck-bending cliffs
the forest and jungle combined to block the sun
dangling from branches snakes looked like grapevines
bandits filled the land wherever I stayed
old and young cried out as they were killed or kidnapped
I didn't stop to eat and kept watch at night
I banged on a drum until my arms ached
the blisters that formed felt like wounds
somehow I managed to escape death's grasp
and now I've contracted cholera
my insides feel like I swallowed a knife
I'm weaker and my body is nothing but bones
and my hair has suddenly turned white
I know you've been busy and were banished too
I've tried to write but I'm out of lines
the royal forces have defeated the rebels
there's no place a cool breeze doesn't blow
if imperial grace should ever reach these roadside weeds
after ten years of being trampled I'm exhausted
at least I escaped the nets meant for prey
and I'm ending my journey by the sea
having accomplished nothing but adding years to this body
when I look northeast my heart aches

初拜柳州出東郊，道旁相送皆賢豪。迴眸炫晃別群玉，獨赴異域穿蓬蒿。
炎煙六月咽口鼻，胸鳴肩舉不可逃。桂州西南又千里，漓水鬭石麻蘭高。
陰森野葛交蔽日，懸蛇結虺如蒲萄。到官數宿賊滿野，縛壯殺老啼且號。

饑行夜坐設方略，籠銅枹鼓手所操。奇瘡釘骨狀如箭，鬼手脫命爭纖毫。
今年噬毒得霍疾，支心攪腹戟與刀。邇來氣少筋骨露，蒼白潷汩盈顛毛。
君今砣砣又竄逐，辭賦已復窮詩騷。神兵廟略頻破虜，四溟不日清風濤。
聖恩儻忽念行葦，十年踐踏久已勞。幸因解網入鳥獸，畢命江海終遊遨。
願言未果身益老，起望東北心滔滔。

....

NOTE: Written in Liuchou in the fall of 817, two years after the events out-
lined in the first half of the poem. Liu left Ch'ang-an in the middle of the
third month of 815 and arrived at his new place of exile at the end of the sixth
month, a journey of over three months, as opposed to the month or so it took
him to travel from Yungchou to the capital at the end of his first exile. Wei
Heng was a younger man, a graduate of the 805 imperial exam and among
those who saw Liu off in 815 on his second exile. The normal place for doing
that was 10 kilometers east of the city at a pavilion that overlooked the Pa
River. Not long after Liu left, Wei Heng was also exiled, in his case to the
Great Wall in northeast China. Near the end of the poem, Liu notes that the
Huaihsi Rebellion, which began in the summer of 814, has finally been put
down: this occurred in the summer of 817. Despite his own predicament, Liu
couldn't stop thinking about the country. (1141)

136. Planting Orange Trees at the Northwest Corner of Liuchou 柳州城西北隅種柑樹

With my own hands I planted 200 orange trees
come spring their new leaves should fill this part of town
like other Ch'u exiles I love these noble trees
the tree servants of Chingchou weren't on my mind
before long they'll blossom and spread their snowy scent
but who will be here to pick their hanging fruit
if I can just wait until they form a grove
their juice might keep this old man alive

手種黃柑二百株，春來新葉徧城隅。方同楚客憐皇樹，不學荊州利木奴。
幾歲開花聞噴雪，何人摘實見垂珠。若教坐待成林日，滋味還堪養老夫。

....

NOTE: Written in Liuchou in the fall of 817. The poet Ch'u Yuan (340–278 BC) was another Ch'u exile who planted orange trees. During the T'ang, the region south of the Yangtze, formerly occupied by the ancient state of Ch'u, was the court's favorite place to send people it didn't like. In the Yangtze River town of Chingchou, there once was an impoverished man who planted orange trees and told his family someday the trees would become their servants. Everyone laughed, but he eventually became wealthy from the harvest. Naturally, Liu was hoping he wouldn't still be in Liuchou when his trees began producing fruit. After his death the townspeople constructed Orange Scent Pavilion 柑香亭 in his memory. They built it beside the pond he frequented. The pond and the pavilion are still there, not far from the shrine and memorial grave they built in his honor. (1182)

XX. CAMEL KUO, THE TREE PLANTER 種樹郭橐駝傳

No one knows Camel Kuo's original name. He was afflicted with a hunched back and walked with his head bent down like a dromedary, so people in his hometown called him "Camel." When Camel heard this, he said, "Excellent! That's a perfect name for me." So he stopped using his real name and called himself Camel. The place where he lived was Fengle County just west of Ch'ang-an. Camel supported himself by planting trees, and all the fruit vendors in Ch'ang-an and wealthy people with an interest in beautiful landscapes vied to hire him to help with their gardens. They noticed that any of the trees Camel planted or transplanted not only survived but flourished and produced their fruit earlier. Other gardeners watched what he did and tried to copy him, but without success.

When someone asked him about this, Camel replied, "I can't make a tree live forever or even flourish, but I can accord with a tree's inherent characteristics so that it manifests its nature, that's all. The essential thing in planting a tree is for the roots to be spread out, for the mound to be level, for the soil to be old, and for the tamping to be firm. Beyond that, I don't touch it or worry about it but just leave it alone. If you plant it as if it were a young child, then ignore it as if it were trash, it will develop all of its inherent characteristics and manifest its nature. I just don't interfere with its development, that's all. I can't make it flourish, and I can't make it thrive, and I can't make it produce its fruit any earlier. Other gardeners aren't like this: they pack the roots and loosen the soil and in mounding it up either add too much or not enough. Even if they can avoid these things, they show it too much attention and worry about it too much, and they keep checking on it day and night. In extreme cases, they scratch the bark to see if it's alive, or they shake the trunk to see if it's loose, and the tree gets further away from its nature. They say they love it but end up hurting it. They say they worry about it but end up injuring it—so they aren't like me. But what can I do about that?"

The same person then asked, "Can your method be extended to the management of government?" Camel said, "I only know how to plant trees. Managing isn't my trade. But since I've been living in this county, I've seen officials giving all kinds of orders as if they loved the people but in the end causing them grief. Morning and night their runners come around and shout, 'The chief orders you to hurry up with the plowing,' or 'Get on with the planting,' or 'Look to the harvest,' or 'Hurry and soak the silkworms and unreel the silk,' or 'Hurry and weave the thread,' or 'Teach your children how to read,' or 'Watch the pigs and chickens.' They pound their drums and beat their boards to summon us. We have to feed and entertain these lackeys and have little time for ourselves. How are we supposed to survive, much less enjoy our lives? Thus we get sick and wear ourselves out. That's how it is with anyone in my trade."

The man exclaimed, "Is this not marvelous? I asked about taking care of trees, and I learned about the art of taking care of the people." And so I'm passing this on as a warning to officials.

郭橐駝，不知始何名。病瘻，隆然伏行，有類橐駝，故鄉人號之駝。駝聞之曰甚善，名我固當。因捨其名，亦自謂橐駝云。其鄉曰豐樂鄉，在長安西。駝業種樹，凡長安豪富人為觀遊及賣果者，皆爭迎取養。視駝所種樹，或移徙，無不活，且碩茂早實以蕃。他植者雖窺伺傚慕，莫能如也。

有問之，對曰橐駝非能使木壽且孳也，能順木之天，以致其性焉爾。凡植木之性，其本欲舒，其培欲平，其土欲故，其築欲密。既然已，勿動勿慮，去不復顧。其蒔也若子，其置也若棄，則其天者全而其性得矣。故吾不害其長而已，非有能碩而茂之也，不抑耗其實而已，非有能早而蕃之也。他植者則不然，根拳而土易，其培之也，若不過焉則不及。苟有能反是者，則又愛之太恩，憂之太勤，旦視而暮撫，已去而復顧。甚者瓜其膚以驗其生枯，搖其本以觀其疏密，而木之性日以離矣。雖曰愛之，其實害之，雖曰憂之，其實讎之，故不我若也。吾又何能為哉。

問者曰以子之道，移之官理可乎。駝曰我知種樹而已，理，非吾業也。然吾居鄉，見長人者好煩其令，若甚憐焉，而卒以禍。旦暮吏來而呼曰，官命促爾耕，勗爾植，督爾穫，早繅而緒，早織而縷，字而幼孩，遂而雞豚。鳴鼓而聚之，擊木而召之。吾小人輟飧饔以勞吏者，且不得暇，又何以蕃吾生而安吾性耶。故病且怠。若是，則與吾業者其亦有類乎。

問者曰噫，不亦善夫。吾問養樹，得養人術。傳其事以為官戒也。　(473)

137. South Office Sent a Notice It Plans to Compile a Watershed Map and Include Local Customs and Stories 南省轉牒欲具江國圖令盡通風俗故事

In ancient times the boundaries were the seas
"wilderness" was listed among "mountains and rivers"
when it was first mentioned in the *Huayitu Record*
the section on customs was left blank
old men with braided hair aren't easy to talk to
they prefer to stay in their huts and caves
but South Palace wants to know these things
maybe there's something in the Chou "Borderland" chapter

聖代提封盡海壖，狼荒猶得紀山川。華夷圖上應初錄，風土記中殊未傳。
椎髻老人難借問，黃茆深峒敢留連。南宮有意求遺俗，試檢周書王會篇。

....

NOTE: Written in Liuchou in 818. The T'ang dynasty's Department of State Affairs was located just outside the south gate of the palace and was referred to as South Office, South Hall, and also South Palace. Liu is responding to the government's request for information about local customs and stories in the "wilderness" that was Liuchou so it could be included in a new national gazetteer. Such information was not in earlier records, including the *Hainei Huayitu* 海內華夷圖 compiled by Chia Tan 賈耽 in 801. Although Liuchou was mentioned in that edition, no information about the area was included. In the last line, Liu says he'll take a look at the Chou-dynasty record of its borderlands, compiled around 350 BC, if only to have a model. (1145)

138. Sent from Liuchou to a Dear Friend in the Capital 柳州寄京中親故

From the Linyi Mountains to the Miasmic Sea it's fall
the Tsangke River flows past the prefectural seat
since you bothered asking Dragon Town's location
north of here Chinchou is three thousand *li* away

林邑山聯瘴海秋，牂牁水向郡前流。勞君遠問龍城地，正北三千到錦州。

....

NOTE: Written in Liuchou in the fall of 818, in response to a question from a friend about Liuchou—or Dragon Town, as it was also known—and its relation to Chinchou. The name Linyi (Forest Capital) was a shortened form of Hsianglinyi 象林邑 (Elephant Forest Capital), the name Chinese gave to a kingdom in central Vietnam. As elsewhere, Liu uses the term to refer to the mountain range that stretches south from Kueilin and Liuchou into Vietnam. The Tsangke (or Liuchiang River) flowed through Liuchou on its way to the South China Sea via the Hsun and West Rivers. The last line is meant as an exaggeration. From Liuchou, Chinchou (near modern Mayang 麻陽) was only 700 *li,* or 350 kilometers to the north. But for him, it may as well have been 3,000 *li,* as he had no hope of ever going that far north, much less all the way to Ch'ang-an. From Chinchou to Ch'ang-an it was another 3,500 *li.* (1184)

139. Waking up Alone 獨覺

The windows were fogged up when I awoke
it was a pitter-patter rainy morning
I hate setting off on a good hike late
but I was overwhelmed by minor tasks
you ask what I think about statecraft
who among the ancients understood it

覺來窗牖空，寥落雨聲曉。良游怨遲暮，末事驚紛擾。
為問經世心，古人誰盡了。

....

NOTE: Six-line poems were rare in the T'ang, but Liu left us three, this being the third. Commentators think it was written in Yungchou. But Liu didn't have any responsibilities in Yungchou. "Minor tasks" and thoughts about "statecraft" sound like Liuchou to me. Perhaps in this case he was simply anxious to go hiking—despite the rain and the job. (1212)

140. Joking about Planting Willows 種柳戲題

Magistrate Willow of Willow Town
planted willows by Willow River
such a play on words might become a story
perhaps one set in the past
with hanging branches shading the ground
and soaring trunks touching the sky
such trees might remind people of me
but alas of no wisdom that improved their lives

柳州柳刺史，種柳柳江邊。談笑為故事，推移成昔年。
垂陰當覆地，聳幹會參天。好作思人樹，慚無惠化傳。

....

NOTE: Written in Liuchou at the beginning of 819. The third line reads as if the first two lines might have become a popular saying in Liuchou (Willow Town) after Liu (Mister Willow) arrived. Commentators suggest the last couplet refers to Duke Chao 召公 (ca. 1000 BC) of the Chou dynasty who conducted his government under a crabapple tree. After he died, people refused to cut down crabapple trees in recognition of the benevolence of his administration. Liu would have been familiar with this story, and it works with the penultimate line. But I suggest he had another story in mind, one that concerns his own ur-ancestor, Chan Huo 展獲 (720–621 BC), who lived in the state of Lu, where Confucius was born two centuries later. Chan Huo sat under a willow and dispensed wise advice, and people started calling him Liu-hsia-hui, or the Wise Man under the Willow. The name stuck, and this marked the beginning of the Liu, or Willow, clan to which Tsung-yuan belonged, a member of its fortieth generation. Although Liu clearly felt he had been a failure as a magistrate, the townspeople disagreed. When he died a few months after he wrote this, they built a shrine in his honor and turned the place where he lived into a park still known for its willows and orange trees. (1171)

Liu Tzu-hou's Epitaph 柳子厚墓誌銘
by Han Yu 韓愈

Tzu-hou's personal name was Tsung-yuan. He was the seventh lineal male descendent of Liu Ch'ing [516–566], who served as a grand councillor during the Northern Wei dynasty and who was enfeoffed as Duke of Chiyin. His great-granduncle, Liu Shih, was a grand councillor during the T'ang but was sentenced to death along with Chu Sui-liang and Han Yuan during the reign of Emperor Kao-tsung for offending Empress Wu. His father, Liu Chen, gave up his post as erudite at the Court of Ceremonials to care for his mother and asked instead to serve as a county magistrate in the Chiangnan region. Later, because he failed to acquiesce to a high official, he lost his position as censor. But upon that man's death, he was promoted to attendant censor and was known for his adherence to principles. He counted among his friends noteworthy men of the time.

As a youth Tzu-hou was precocious, and there was nothing he wasn't interested in. While his father was still alive, he acted like an adult despite his young age, and when he passed the imperial exam, his talents suddenly became evident. People began talking about the Lius' son. Later, he passed a special exam for erudites and received the position of proofreader in the Academy of Scholarly Worthies. He was exceptionally bright and fiercely honest and cited the works of moderns and ancients in his discussions. Conversant with the classics and histories, he was a forceful debater and always outshone those present. As his reputation grew, he became widely admired and sought-out. People of high rank and stature competed to enlist him as their student and outdid each other in their praise.

In the nineteenth year of the Chenyuan period [803], he was promoted from military commissioner of Lantien to investigating censor. When Shun-tsung ascended the throne, he was promoted to vice director of the Ministry of Rites. But because the person who recommended him committed an offense, he was accordingly banished to serve as a magistrate. But before he reached his post, he was further demoted to assistant magistrate of Yungchou. Despite having no official duties, he exerted himself all the more in reading and reciting poetry and prose, whether

superficial or profound, as he explored all genres and rambled among mountains and streams.

During the Yuanho period, he was recalled to the capital but was sent out again as magistrate of Liuchou. Upon his arrival there, he sighed, "Is this place not worthy of a proper administration?" He established regulations and prohibitions concerning local customs that the people accepted. Among the customs was the use of boys and girls as surety for a debt, which, if not repaid in time together with the interest, resulted in their becoming slaves. Tzu-hou established procedures for buying them back. If the debtor was too poor and unable to repay the loan, the creditor recorded their wages until the debt was repaid and the surety returned. The Surveillance Commissioner ordered this method to be used in other counties, and within one year a thousand people were thus redeemed. All the successful exam candidates south of Hengyang viewed Tzu-hou as their teacher. They took whatever methods Tzu-hou used in his instructions as models for their own procedures.

Liu Meng-te [Yu-hsi] of Chungshan was also recalled to the capital and reassigned as a prefect and sent again into exile, this time to Pochou. Tzu-hou cried, "With Pochou not fit for human habitation, and Meng-te's mother still alive, I can't bear the thought of their hardship and haven't the words to explain to her why she and her son should have to go there." He was about to appeal to the court to reconsider and ask that he go to Pochou instead of Liuchou and that he wouldn't mind dying if by doing so he gave offense. Fortunately, someone presented Meng-te's situation to those in charge, and Meng-te's post was changed to Lienchou.

It's unfortunate that it takes adversity for us to see a gentleman's true character. Nowadays, it's common for people who share the same neighborhood and admire one another—who drink and eat and enjoy their time with one another, who laugh together, who hold hands and bare their hearts, and cry before Heaven and vow to die before turning their backs on one another and seem so trustworthy—one day to have some minor conflict no bigger than the hair on their heads, and they look at one another as if they were strangers, and one of them falls into a pit, and the other not only doesn't stretch forth their hand but casts stones on them: and of whom isn't this true? Even animals or barbarians wouldn't dare do such things, but these people consider what they do to be normal. Hearing about Tzu-hou's actions, such people must feel ashamed!

When Tzu-hou was young, he was courageous and didn't put his own interests ahead of others. He thought his achievements would stand on their own, hence he accepted his demotions. But once he was demoted, because those who knew him lacked the influence or position to help him, he died in the wilderness, his talents of no use to the age and his understanding of no help to the world. When Tzu-hou was at court, if he had acted as he did when he was assistant prefect or prefect, he never would have been dismissed. And even when he was dismissed, if others in power had recommended him, he would have been recalled and not banished. But if Tzu-hou hadn't been dismissed for so many years and hadn't been banished so far, even if he had reappeared, his writings without doubt would not have had the power to be passed down to posterity as they have. Even if Tzu-hou had realized his wishes and served as a chief minister for a while, there are certainly those who would have argued about who gained and who lost in exchanging one for the other.

Tzu-hou died on the eighth day of the eleventh month of the fourteenth year of the Yuanhe period [819]. He was forty-seven. On the tenth day of the seventh month of the fifteenth year, he was buried at Wannien [plateau south of Ch'ang-an] alongside the graves of his ancestors. Tzu-hou had two sons. The eldest was Chou-liu, who had just turned four. The youngest was Chou-ch'i, who was born after Tzu-hou died. He also left two young daughters. His burial expenses were paid for by Surveillance Commissioner P'ei Hsing-li of Hotung. A man known for his integrity and generosity and for keeping his word, Hsing-li became friends with Tzu-hou, who treated him with deference and in the end has relied on his efforts. It was Tzu-hou's cousin, Lu Tsun, who buried him at Wannien. Tsun is from Chuochou and is by nature attentive and never tires of learning. Since Tzu-hou was dismissed, Tsun accompanied him as part of his family and stayed with him until his death. After burying Tzu-hou, he also intends to take care of his household affairs—a rare man from beginning to end. The tomb inscription reads:

"This is the grave of Tzu-hou. May its permanence and peace benefit his descendants."

子厚諱宗元。七世祖慶，為拓跋魏侍中，封濟陰公。曾伯祖奭，為唐宰相，與褚遂良、韓瑗俱得罪武后，死高宗朝。皇考諱鎮，以事母棄太常博士，求為縣令江南。其後，以不能媚權貴，失御史。權貴人死，乃復拜侍御史，號為剛直。所與游皆當世名人。

子厚少精敏，無不通達。逮其父時，雖少年，已自成人。能取進士第，嶄然見頭角，眾謂柳氏有子矣。其後以博學宏詞授集賢殿正字。俊傑廉悍，議論證據今古，出入經史百子，踔厲風發，率常屈其座人。名聲大振，一時皆慕與之交。諸公要人爭欲令出我門下，交口薦譽之。

貞元十九年，由藍田尉拜監察御史。順宗即位，拜禮部員外郎。遇用事者得罪，例出為刺史。未至，又例貶永州司馬。居閑，益自刻苦，務記覽，為詞章，汎濫停蓄，為深博無涯涘，而自肆於山水間。

元和中，嘗例召至京師。又偕出為刺史，而子厚得柳州。既至，歎曰是豈不足為政邪。因其土俗，為設教禁，州人順賴。其俗以男女質錢，約不時贖，子本相侔，則沒為奴婢。子厚與設方計，悉令贖歸。其尤貧力不能者，令書其傭，足相當，則使歸其質。觀察使下其法於他州，比一歲，免而歸者且千人。衡湘以南，為進士者，皆以子厚為師。其經承子厚口講指畫為文詞者，悉有法度可觀。

其召至京師而復為刺史也，中山劉夢得禹錫亦在遣中，當詣播州。子厚泣曰播州非人所居，而夢得親在堂，吾不忍夢得之窮，無辭以白其大人，且萬無母子俱往理。請於朝，將拜疏，願以柳易播，雖重得罪，死不恨。遇有以夢得事白上者，夢得於是改刺連州。

嗚呼，士窮乃見節義。今夫平居里巷相慕悅，酒食游戲相徵逐，詡詡強笑語以相取下，握手出肺肝相示，指天日涕泣，誓生死不相背負，真若可信，一旦臨利害，僅如毛髮比，反眼若不相識，落陷穽不一引手救，反擠之，又下石焉者，皆是也。此宜禽獸夷狄所不忍為，而其人自視以為得計，聞子厚之風，亦可以少愧矣。

子厚前時少年，勇于为人，不自贵重顾籍，谓功业可立就，故坐废退。既退，又无相知有气力得位者推挽，故卒死于穷裔。材不为世用，道不行于时也。使子厚在台省时，自持其身，已能如司马刺史时，亦自不斥。斥时，有人力能举之，且必复用不穷。然子厚斥不久，穷不极，虽有出于人，其文学辞章，必不能自力，以致必传于后如今，无疑也。虽使子厚得所愿，为将相于一时，以彼易此，孰得孰失，必有能辨之者。

子厚前時少年，勇於為人，不自貴重顧藉，謂功業可立就，故坐廢退。既退，又無相知有氣力得位者推挽，故卒死於窮裔，材不為世用，道不行於時也。使子厚在臺省時，自持其身已能如司馬刺史時，亦自不斥。斥時，有人力能舉之，且必復用不窮。然自厚斥不久，窮不極，雖有出於人，其文學辭章，必不能自力以致必傳於後如今無疑也。雖使子厚得所願，為將相於一時，以彼易此，孰得孰失，必有能辨之者。

子厚以元和十四年十一月八日卒，年四十七。以十五年七月十日歸葬萬年先人墓側。子厚有子男二人，長曰周六，始四歲，季曰周七，子厚卒乃生。女子二人，皆幼。其得歸葬也，費皆出觀察使河東裴君行立。行立有節概，重然諾，與子厚結交，子厚亦為之盡，竟賴其力。葬子厚於萬年之墓者，舅弟盧遵。遵，涿人，性謹慎，學問不厭。自子厚之斥，遵從而家焉，逮其死不去。既往葬子厚，又將經紀其家，庶幾有始終者。

銘曰是惟子厚之室。既固既安，以利其嗣人。（1434）

Lexicon

The following list includes the modified Wade-Giles romanization used in this book for Chinese names, terms, and places (note that I omit the usual apostrophes and hyphens for place names), followed by the Pinyin romanization, currently in vogue in China, and finally the traditional Chinese characters.

Academy of Scholarly Worthies / 集賢殿書院

ai-nai / *ai-nai* / 欸乃

An Lu-shan / An Lushan / 安祿山

Analects / 論語

Censorate / 御史臺

Chan Huo / Zhang Huo / 展獲

Chang Chien-feng / Zhang Jianfeng / 張建封

Chang Chih / Zhang Zhi / 張芝

Chang Chiu-ling / Zhang Jiuling / 張九齡

Chang Heng / Zhang Heng / 張衡

Chang Yi / Zhang Yi / 張毅

Ch'ang-an / Chang'an / 長安

Changchou / Zhangzhou / 漳州

Changsha / Changsha / 長沙

Changte / Changde / 常德

Changwu / Changwu / 長烏

Chao (state, surname) / Zhao / 趙

Chao Meng / Zhao Meng / 趙孟

Chaoyang / Chaoyang / 朝陽

Ch'ao-fu / Chaofu / 巢父

Ch'en (river) / Chen / 溱

Ch'en Lien / Chen Lian / 陳諫

Ch'en Teng / Chen Deng / 陳登

Ch'en Tzu-ang / Chen Zi'ang / 陳子昂

Chen-hu / Zhenhu / 鍼虎

Chen-yi / Zhenyi / 貞一

Chenchou / Chenzhou / 郴州

Cheng (river) / Zheng / 蒸

Chi K'ang / Qi Kang / 嵇康

Chia P'eng / Jia Peng / 賈鵬

Chia Tan / Jia Dan / 賈耽

Chia Yi / Jia Yi / 賈誼

Chianghua / Jianghua / 江華

Chiangling / Jiangling / 江陵

Chienchiuling / Qianqiuling / 千秋嶺

Chifeng / Qifeng / 棲鳳

Chih Shih-ch'i / Zhi Shiqi / 酈食其

Chih Tao-lin / Zhi Daolin / 支道林

Chih Tun / Zhi Dun / 支遁

Chih-yi / Zhiyi / 智顗

245

Chin (dynasty, state) / Jin / 晉

Ch'in (dynasty, state) / Qin / 秦

Chinchou / Jinzhou / 錦州

Chingchou / Jingzhou / 荊州

Chingmen / Jingmen / 荊門

Chingshui (river) / Qingshui /
清水

Chinjen (ward) / Qinren / 親仁

Chiuyi (mountain) / Jiuyi / 九疑

Ch'i (state) / Qi / 齊

chou / zhou / 州

Chou (dynasty, surname) / Zhou
/ 周

Chou Chi / Zhou Ji / 騶忌

Chou Chun-ch'ao / Zhou
Junchao / 周君巢

Choushan (islands) / Zhoushan /
舟山

Chu-ke Liang / Zhuge Liang /
諸葛亮

Chuang (tribe) / Zhuang / 壯

Chuang-tzu (book, name) /
Zhuangzi / 莊子

Chueh-chao / Juezhao / 覺照

Chung Yao / Zhong Yao / 鍾繇

Chung-hsing / Zhongxing / 仲行

Ch'ung-sun / Chongsun / 重異

Chungling / Chongling / 春陵

Chungnan (mountains) /
Zhongnan / 終南山

Ch'u (region, state) / Chu / 楚

Ch'u Po-yu / Qu Boyu / 蘧伯玉

Ch'u Yuan / Qu Yuan / 屈原

Ch'un Yu / Chun Yu / 淳于

Confucius / 孔子

Department of State Affairs /
尚書省

Duke Chao / Zhao / 召公

Duke Hsuan / Xuan / 宣公

Duke Huan / Huan / 桓公

Duke K'ang / Kang / 康公

Duke Mu / Mu / 穆公

Duke of Chou / Zhou / 周公

Duke Shao / Shao / 召公

Eight Assistant Magistrates /
八司馬

Emperor Hsien-tsung / Xianzong /
憲宗

Emperor Huang / Huang / 黃帝

Emperor Kuang-wu / Guangwu /
光武帝

Emperor Shun / Shun / 舜帝

Emperor Shun-tsung / Shunzong
/ 順宗

Emperor Te-tsung / Dezong /
德宗

Emperor Wu / Wu / 武帝

Emperor Yao / Yao / 堯

Emperor Yuan / Yuan / 元帝

Empress Hu / 胡太后

Empress Wang / Wang / 王皇后

Fahua (temple) / Fahua / 法華

Fan Ch'eng-ta / Fan Chengda /
范成大

Fan Chung / Fan Chong / 樊重

Fanyang / Fanyang / 范陽

Feng (river) / Feng / 灃

Feng Hsu / Feng Xu / 馮敘

fu / *fu* / 賦

Fu Hsi / Fu Xi / 伏羲

Fuchun (river) / Fuchun / 富春江

Ha / Ha / 哈

Hainei Huayitu / *Hainei Huayitu* / 海內華夷圖

Han (dynasty, river) / Han / 漢

Han T'ai / Han Tai / 韓泰

Han Yeh / Han Ye / 韓曄

Han Yu / Han Yu / 韓愈

Han-shan / Hanshan / 寒山

Hangchou / Hangzhou / 杭州

Hankou / Hankou / 漢口

Hanku (pass) / Hangu / 函谷關

Hanlin / Hanlin / 翰林

Hantan / Handan / 邯鄲

Hanyang / Hanyang / 潢陽

Hao-ch'u / Haochu / 浩初

Heart Sutra / 心經

Heng / Heng / 哼

Hengchou / Hengzhou / 衡州

Hengshan / Hengshan / 衡山/岳

Hengyang / Hengyang / 衡陽

Ho-niang / Honiang / 和娘

Ho-tung / Hedong / 河東

Hsiang (county) / Xiang / 象

Hsiang (river) / Xiang / 湘

Hsiang Hsiu / Xiang Xiu / 向秀

Hsianglinyi / Xianglinyi / 象林邑

Hsiangssu (canal) / Xiangsi / 相思

Hsiangyang / Xiangyang / 襄陽

Hsiao (river) / Xiao / 瀟

Hsiaohsiang / Xiaoxiang / 瀟湘

Hsiaokuan (pass) / Xiaoguan / 崤關

Hsichuan / Xichuan / 西川

Hsieh An / Xie An / 謝安

Hsieh T'iao / Xie Tiao / 謝朓

Hsienjenshan / Xianrenshan / 仙人山

Hsienyang / Xianyang / 咸陽

Hsinglu (ward) / Xinglu / 興祿

Hsu Chun / Xu Jun / 徐俊

Hsu Er / Xu Er / 徐二

Hsu Hsia-k'o / Xu Xiake / 徐霞客

Hsuancheng / Xuancheng / 宣城

Hsuanchou / Xuanzhou / 宣州

Hsuanpu / Xuanpu / 玄圃

Hsuchou / Xuzhou / 徐州

Hsun (river) / Xun / 潯

Hua T'uo / Hua Tuo / 花佗

Huai (river) / Huai / 淮

Huaihsi / Huaixi / 淮西

Huainan / Huainan / 淮南

Huang (river) / Huang / 黃溪

Huang Pa / Huang Ba / 黃霸

Hui-lin / Huilin / 惠林

Hui-neng / Huineng / 蕙能

Hui-yuan / Huiyuan / 慧遠

Hun Chien / Hun Jian / 渾鍼

Hundred Family Shoals / 百家瀨

Janhsi / Ranxi / 冉溪

Juan Chi / Ruan Ji / 阮籍

Jungchou / Rongzhou / 容州

Jungchou / Rongzhou / 融州

Junghsien / Rongxian / 容縣

Kaiyuan (temple) / Kaiyuan / 開元

k'ai-shu / kaishu / 開書

Kan (river) / Gan / 贛

Kao-tsung / Gaozong / 高宗

Kaoshan / Gaoshan / 高山

Kaoyang / Gaoyang / 高陽

Koulou / Goulou / 岣嶁

ku-wen / gu-wen / 古文

K'ua-fu / Kuafu / 夸父

Kuan (river) / Guan / 灌

Kuan-nu / Guan'nu / 官奴

Kuei (river, region) / Gui / 桂

Kueichou / Guizhou / 桂州

Kueilin / Guilin / 桂林

Kueiling / Guiling / 桂嶺

Kueiyang / Guiyang / 桂陽

Kung-ku / Gonggu/ 龔古

Kunlun / Kunlun / 崑崙

Kunming / Kunming / 崑明

Ladies of the Hsiang / 湘妃

Langchou / Langzhou / 郎州

Lantien / Lantian / 藍田

Lanting / Lanting / 蘭亭

Lao-tzu / Laozi / 老子

li (distance) / *li* / 里

Li (river) / Li / 漓

Li Chi-fu / Li Jifu / 李吉甫

Li Ching-lien / Li Jinglian / 李景儉

Li Ch'un / Li Chun / 李純

Li Hsi-ch'uan / Li Xichuan / 李西川

Li Pai / Li Bai / 李白

Li Sung / Li Song / 李誦

Li Xin / 李昕

Li Yi-chien / Li Yijian / 李夷簡

Li You-ch'ing / Li Youqing / 李幼清

li-shu / lishu / 隸書

Liang (state) / Liang / 梁

Liehtzu / Liezi / 列子

lien / lian / 連

Lienchou / Lianzhou / 連州

Lincheng/ Lincheng / 臨蒸

Linchuan / Linchuan / 臨川

ling / ling / 嶺

Ling Lun / Ling Lun / 伶倫

Ling-ch'e / Lingche / 靈徹

Lingchu / Lingqu / 靈渠

Lingling / Lingling / 零陵

Lingnan / Lingnan / 嶺南

Lingpao / Lingbao / 靈寶

Linyi / Linyi / 林邑

Linyuan / Linyuan / 臨源

Liu Ch'a-kung / Liu Chagong / 柳察躬

Liu Chen / Liu Zhen / 柳鎮

Liu Ling / Liu Ling / 劉伶

Liu Meng-te / Liu Mengde / 劉夢得

Liu Pang / Liu Bang / 劉邦

Liu Shih / Liu Shi / 柳奭

Liu Tsung-chih / Liu Zongzhi / 柳宗直

Liu Tsung-hsuan / Liu Zongxuan / 柳宗玄

Liu Tsung-yi / Liu Zongyi / 柳宗一

Liu Tsung-yu / Liu Congyu / 柳從裕

Liu Tsung-yuan / Liu Zongyuan / 柳宗元

Liu Yi / Liu Yi / 柳毅

Liu Yu-hsi / Liu Yuxi / 劉禹錫

Liu Yun / Liu Yun / 柳惲

Liu-hsia-hui / Liuxiahui / 柳下惠

Liuchiang / Liujiang / 柳江

Liuchou / Liuzhou / 柳州

Lou Shih-te / Lou Shide / 婁師德

Lou T'u-nan / Lou Tunan / 婁圖南

Loyang / Luoyang / 洛陽

Lu (state) / Lu / 魯

Lu K'ai / Lu Kai / 陸凱

Lu Tsun / Lu Zun / 盧遵

Lu Wen / Lu Wen / 呂溫

Lukou / Lukou / 淥口

Lung An-hai / Long Anhai / 龍安海

Lungcheng / Longcheng / 龍城

Lunghsing (temple) / Longxing / 龍興

Lushan / Lushan / 廬山

Ma Yuan / Ma Yuan / 馬授

Malingshan / Malingshan / 馬嶺山

Mayang / Mayang / 麻陽

Mayuan / Mayuan / 麻園

Meiling / Meiling / 梅嶺

Mencius (book, name) / Mengzi / 孟子

Miao (tribe) / Miao / 苗

Miaomenkou / Miaomenkou / 廟門口

Milo (river) / Miluo / 汨羅

Ming (dynasty) / Ming / 明

Nanching / Nanjing / 南京

Nanling / Nanling / 南嶺

Northern Wci / 北魏

Oshan / Eshan / 峨山

Pa (river) / Ba / 灞

Pai Chu-yi / Bai Juyi / 白居易

Paisha / Baisha / 白沙

Pan Ku / Ban Gu / 班固

pang / *bang* / 邦

Pao Chao / Bao Zhao / 鮑照

P'ei Hsing-li / Pei Xingli / 裴行立

P'ei Tu / Pei Du / 裴度

Penglai / Penglai / 蓬萊

P'eng-tsu / Pengzu / 彭祖

p'ien-wen / *pianwen* / 駢文

Pin (state) / Bin / 豳

Pinchou / Binzhou / 豳州

Pingchou / Pingzhou / 萍州

Pingyin / Pingyin / 平陰

Pintao / Bindao / 頻島

Po-yi / Boyi / 伯夷

Pu Tzu-hsia / Bu Zixia / 卜子夏

Puchou / Puzhou / 蒲洲

Puning / Puning / 普寧

Pupan / Puban / 蒲坂

Rock Channel / 石渠

Rock Creek / 石澗

sao / *sao* / 騷

Shanghai / Shanghai / 上海

Shangshan / Shangshan / 商山

Shanho (ward) / Shanhe / 善和

Shanhsueh / Shanxue / 善謔

Shanyang / Shanyang / 山陽

Shaochou (Hunan) / Shaozhou / 邵州

Shaochou(Kuangtung)/Shaozhou/ 韶州

Shaohsing / Shaoxing / 紹興

Shaokuan / Shaoguan / 韶館

Shaoling (plateau) / Shaoling / 少陵

Shaoyang / Shaoyang / 邵陽

Shen Nung / Shen Nong / 神農

shih (poetry) / *shi* / 詩

Shih-ching / *Shijing* / 詩經

Shihchiao / Shijiao / 石角

Shu-chi / Shuji / 恕己

Shu-ch'i / Shuqi / 叔齊

Shuang / Shuang / 瀧

Ssu-ma Ch'ien / Sima Qian / 司馬遷

Su (river) / Su / 涑

Su Tan / Su Dan / 蘇耽

Su Tung-p'o / Su Dongpo / 蘇東坡

Su Wu / Su Wu / 蘇武

Suchou / Suzhou / 蘇州

Sung (dynasty) / Song / 宋

Suo Ching / Suo Jing / 索靖

Tai-tsung / Daizong / 代宗

Taiping (gate) / Taiping / 太平

Taishan / Taishan / 泰山

Tan Pao / Dan Bao / 單豹

Tanchou / Tanzhou / 潭州

T'ang (dynasty) / Tang / 唐

T'ang Ch'eng-yuan / Tang Chengyuan / 湯澄源

T'ao Yuan-ming / Tao Yuanming / 陶淵明

Taochou / Daozhou / 道州

Taoteching / *Daodejing* / 道德經

Tayuling (pass) / Dayuling / 大庾嶺

Teching / Deqing / 德清

Tienchu / Tianzhu / 天柱

Tou Ch'ang / Dou Chang / 竇常

Tou Shen / Dou Shen / 竇參

Tsangke / Cangke / 牂牁

Tsangwu / Cangwu / 蒼梧

Tsao Chih / Cao Zhi / 曹植

Ts'ao Mo / Cao Mo / 曹沫

ts'ao-shu / *cao-shu* / 草書

Tseng-tzu / Zengzi / 曾子

Tsochuan / *Zuozhuan* / 左傳

Ts'ui Chien / Cui Jian / 崔簡

Ts'ui Min / Cui Min / 崔敏

Ts'ui Ts'e / Cui Ce / 崔策

Tu Fu / Du Fu / 杜甫

Tu Mu / Du Mu / 杜牧

Tuan Chiu / Duan Jiu / 段九

Tuan Hung-ku / Duan Honggu / 段弘古

Tung (tribe) / Dong / 侗

Tung-fang Shuo / Dongfang Shuo / 東方朔

Tungfu / Dongfu / 洞府

Tungshan / Dongshan / 東山

Tungting (lake) / Dongting / 洞庭湖

Tzu-hou / Zihou / 子厚

Tzupo / Zibo / 淄博

Visualization of Paradise Sutra / 觀無量壽佛經

Wang Chun / Wang Jun / 王濬

Wang Hsi-chih / Wang Xizhi / 王羲之

Wang Mang / Wang Mang / 王莽

Wang Shu-wen / Wang Shuwen / 王叔文

Wei (dynasty, state) / Wei / 魏

Wei (river in Honan) / Wei / 洧

Wei (river near Ch'ang-an) / Wei / 渭

Wei Heng / Wei Heng / 韋珩

Wei Hsia-ch'ing / Wei Xiaqing / 韋夏卿

Wei Kuan / Wei Guan / 衛瓘

Wei Kuan-chih / Wei Guanzhi / 韋貫之

Wei Piao / Wei Biao / 韋彪

Wei Shuo / Wei Shuo / 衛鑠

Wei Tao-an / Wei Dao'an / 韋道安

Wei Ying-wu / Wei Yingwu / 韋應物

Wu (state) / Wu / 吳

Wu (tributary) / Wu / 浯

Wu Chao / Wu Zhao / 武曌

Wu Wu-ling / Wu Wuling / 吳武陵

Wu Yuan-heng / Wu Yuanheng / 武元衡

Wuchou / Wuzhou / 梧州

Wukuan / Wuguan / 武關

Yang Hua / Yang Hua / 楊花

Yang P'ing / Yang Ping / 楊凭

Yang Shih-yi / Yang Shiyi / 楊拾遺

Yang Yu-ling / Yang Yuling / 楊於陵

Yangtze / Yangzi / 長江

Yao (tribe) / Yao / 瑤

Yeh Ch'ang / Ye Chang / 冶長

Yen (state) / Yan / 燕

Yen Hui / Yan Hui / 顏回

Yen Tzu-ling / Yan Ziling / 嚴子陵

Yen Ying / Yan Ying / 晏嬰

Yen-hsi / Yanxi / 奄息

yi / *yi* / 益

Yiching (Book of Changes) / *Yijing* / 易經

Yin Hsien / Yin Xian / 殷賢

Yin Yun / 殷雲

Ying / Ying / 郢

Yu (the Great) / Yu / 禹

Yu An-hsi / Yu Anxi / 庾安西

Yuan Chen / Yuan Zhen / 元稹
Yuan Chieh / Yuan Jie / 元結
Yuan K'e-chi / Yuan Keji / 元克己
Yuanho / Yuanhe / 元和
Yueh (state) / Yue / 越
Yueh Yi / Yue Yi / 樂毅

Yuhsi (river) / Yuxi / 愚溪
Yukungku / Yugonggu / 愚公谷
Yungchi / Yongji / 永濟
Yungchou / Yongzhou / 永州
Yungtung / Yongdong / 甬東

Bibliography

Nearly everything in English about Liu Tsung-yuan concerns his prose. As far as I know, the only poems of his that have been translated into English are five poems in *Three Hundred Poems of the T'ang* and less than a dozen in H.C. Chang's work listed below. No doubt, there are a few missed. The following list of Chinese texts includes only those used by the translator and is far from exhaustive. As Liu Tsung-yuan is considered a major literary figure in China, there are dozens of articles in print and online dealing with various aspects of his poetry and his prose. Other than the two titles listed below by William Nienhauser, there is nothing in English that goes into any depth.

English

Chinese Classical Prose: The Eight Masters of the T'ang-Sung Period, by Shih Shun Liu, Hong Kong: Chinese University Press, 1979. Includes a selection of prose pieces; pages 99–132.

Chinese Literature 2, Nature Poetry, by H.C. Chang, New York: Columbia University Press, 1977. Includes translations of a dozen poems or parts of poems; pages 97–124.

The Indiana Companion to Traditional Chinese Literature, edited and compiled by William Nienhauser, Taipei: Southern Materials Center, 1986. Short critical appraisal of Liu Tsung-yuan and his work; pages 589–592.

Liu Tsung-yuan, by William Nienhauser, Charles Hartman, et al., New York: Twayne Publishers, 1973. This remains the only comprehensive source of information in English about Liu Tsung-yuan.

Poetry and Prose of the Tang and Song, translated by Yang Xianyi and Gladys Yang, Beijing: Chinese Literature Press (Panda Books), 1984. Includes a selection of prose pieces; pages 135–179,

Chinese

[An appreciation and analysis of Liu Tsung-yuan's Yungchou poetry] 柳宗元永州詩歌賞析, edited by Lu Guokang 呂國康 and Yang Jinzhuan

楊金磚, Changsha: Hunan Culture & Arts Publishing Company 湖南文藝出版社, 2002. Lu Guokang is a retired professor and resident of Yungchou who has specialized in the study of Liu Tsung-yuan and his poetry and prose.

[The collected works of Liu Tsung-yuan] 柳宗元集, Beijing: China Publishing Company 中華書局, 1979. This is currently the standard edition of the poems and the edition on which I have based my translations.

[Focus on Yungchou] 關注永州, by Cai Zixin 蔡自新, Zhuhai: Zhuhai Publishing Company 洙海出版社, 2008. A useful source of background information about Yungchou.

[Liu Tsung-yuan, a discussion & appraisal] 柳宗元評說, by Lu Guo-kang 呂國康, Nanning: Guangxi People's Publishing Company 廣西人民出版社, 2008.

[Liu Tsung-yuan anthology] 柳宗元集, selected and edited by Shang Yong-liang 尚永亮 and Hong Yinhua 洪迎華, Nanjing: Fenghuang Publishing Company 鳳凰出版社, 2014. A useful edition with a good selection of Liu Tsung-yuan's poetry and prose with accompanying commentary.

[A Liu Tsung-yuan compendium] 柳宗元大辭典, edited by Wu Wenzhi 吳文治 and Xie Hanchang 謝漢強, Huangshan: Huangshan Press, 黃山書社, 2004. This remains the most comprehensive volume, published to date, of information about all aspects of Liu Tsung-yuan—including the people he knew and his works, both the poetry and the prose.

[Liu Tsung-yuan face-to-face] 柳宗元面面觀, by Wang Yimin 王一民, Nanning: Guangxi People's Publishing Company 廣西人民出版社, 2011. One of the few sources that focus on Liu Tsung-yuan's time in Liuchou.

[Liu Tsung-yuan's traces in Yungchou and discussion of his poetry and prose] 柳宗元永州事跡與詩文考論, by Di Mangui 翟滿桂, Shanghai: Shanghai Sanlien Bookstore 上海三聯書店, 2015.

[Liu Tsung-yuan, teacher of a dynasty] 一代宗師柳宗元, by Di Mangui 翟滿桂, Changsha: Yuelu Press 岳麓書社, 2002. Professor Di is a native of Yungchou who has devoted herself to researching the work of Liu Tsung-yuan.

[Liu Tsung-yuan: teaching & study of his poetry and prose] 柳宗元詩文教與學, by Lu Guo-kang 呂國康, Zhuhai: Zhuhai Publishing Company 珠海出版社, 2004.

[Regional culture of Yungchou] 永州地域文化, edited by Chen Hong 陈弘, Zhuhai: Guangming Daily Publishing Company 光明日报出版社, 2016. Another worthwhile source of information about Yungchou.

Bill Porter was born in Van Nuys, California, on October 3, 1943, and grew up in northern Idaho, where his parents moved in 1954. Since his father was often away on business, Porter attended boarding schools in Los Angeles and San Francisco, where he graduated from high school in 1961. After a tour of duty in the US Army (1964–67), he attended UC Santa Barbara and majored in anthropology. In 1970, he entered graduate school at Columbia University and studied anthropology with a faculty that included Margaret Mead and Ruth Benedict. While he was living in New York, he became interested in Buddhism, and in 1972 he left America and moved to a Buddhist monastery in Taiwan. After more than three years with the monks and nuns, he struck out on his own and supported himself by teaching English and later by working as a journalist at English-language radio stations in Taiwan and Hong Kong. During this time, he married a Chinese woman, with whom he has two children, and began working on translations of Chinese poetry and Buddhist texts. In 1993, he returned to America so that his children could learn English, and he has lived ever since in Port Townsend, Washington. For the past twenty years, he has worked as an independent scholar and has supported himself from book royalties and speaking fees. He has given talks on Zen at dozens of Zen centers throughout the United States and has lectured on Chinese history, culture, religion, and poetry at many of the major universities in the United States, England, and Germany. His translations of texts related to these subjects have been honored with a number of awards, including two NEA translation fellowships, a PEN translation award, the inaugural Asian Literature Award of the American Literary Translators Association, a Guggenheim Fellowship, and the Thorton Wilder Translation Prize given by the American Academy of Arts and Letters.

Poetry is vital to language and living. Since 1972, Copper Canyon Press has published extraordinary poetry from around the world to engage the imaginations and intellects of readers, writers, booksellers, librarians, teachers, students, and donors.

WE ARE GRATEFUL FOR THE MAJOR SUPPORT PROVIDED BY:

THE PAUL G. ALLEN
FAMILY FOUNDATION

Anonymous

Jill Baker and Jeffrey Bishop

Anne and Geoffrey Barker

Donna and Matt Bellew

John Branch

Diana Broze

The Beatrice R. and Joseph A. Coleman Foundation Inc.

The Currie Family Fund

Laurie and Oskar Eustis

Mimi Gardner Gates

Nancy Gifford

Gull Industries Inc. on behalf of William True

The Trust of Warren A. Gummow

Carolyn and Robert Hedin

Bruce Kahn

Phil Kovacevich and Eric Wechsler

Lakeside Industries Inc.
on behalf of Jeanne Marie Lee

TO LEARN MORE ABOUT UNDERWRITING
COPPER CANYON PRESS TITLES,
PLEASE CALL 360-385-4925 EXT. 103

WE ARE GRATEFUL FOR THE MAJOR SUPPORT PROVIDED BY:

Maureen Lee and Mark Busto
Peter Lewis
Ellie Mathews and Carl Youngmann as The North Press
Hank Meijer
Gregg Orr
Petunia Charitable Fund and adviser Elizabeth Hebert
Gay Phinny
Suzie Rapp and Mark Hamilton
Emily and Dan Raymond
Jill and Bill Ruckelshaus
Cynthia Sears
Kim and Jeff Seely
Richard Swank
Dan Waggoner
Barbara and Charles Wright
Caleb Young as C. Young Creative
The dedicated interns and faithful volunteers
of Copper Canyon Press

The Chinese character for poetry is made up
of two parts: "word" and "temple."
It also serves as pressmark for
Copper Canyon Press.

This book is set in Minion Pro with
Chinese in Sim Sun. Display type set
in Minion Pro Medium and Minion Pro Medium Display,
with sans serif details in Meta OT Regular.
Book design by Gopa & Ted2, Inc.
Printed on archival-quality paper.